# FOUNDATIONS OF JAVA PROGRAMMING

## FOR THE OBJECT-ORIENTED PROGRAMMING OPTION

## OF THE INTERNATIONAL BACCALAUREATE

## COMPUTER SCIENCE EXAM

Călin Galeriu, Ph.D.

ISBN 978-1-4478-7353-2

Imprint: Lulu.com

# TABLE OF CONTENTS

# Introduction

During the 2017-1018 school year I taught Computer Science (CS) at the Mark Twain International School in Romania. It was a small class of high school students preparing to take the International Baccalaureate (IB) exams in May 2019. The Computer Science Option selected by these students was Object-Oriented Programming, which is usually taught based on computer programming in Java. On this occasion I discovered that there were no good teaching resources specifically tailored for this task. The Java textbooks on the market were huge books with hundreds of pages covering a lot of material that was not needed for the IB CS exam. Students preparing for the comprehensive IB exams may not have the extra time to study advanced programming topics like Java applets, graphics, or anything else not included in the IB CS curriculum. What was even worse, I found that many Java programs presented in these books were very long, often going on and on over several pages. While professional programmers would have no trouble dissecting such computer programs, I was afraid that many high school students would find themselves on a very steep learning curve, with negative effects on their self-confidence and motivation. I personally believe that an introduction to any programming language has to be based on short programs, short enough that the students will type all of these programs with their own hands, line by line, before compiling and executing them. This educational philosophy, this teaching strategy, closely mirrors the best practice of requiring the students to copy in their notebooks all the information written by the teacher on the whiteboard. When the information travels on this path from the whiteboard to the notebook, going through the students' eyes, brains, arms, and hands, this is when the information is being processed, this is when active learning takes place. I therefore decided to write my own class notes, an introduction to the Java programming language based on short Java programs, each one of them no longer than a single page (with the exception of just one longer program at the end of this book). Of course, once the Java programming concepts are fully mastered with the help of the short Java programs from this book, the students are encouraged to continue to improve their computer science and Java programming skills with the help of other textbooks that make use of longer and more complex Java programs. To facilitate future growth, I also included in this textbook a few Java topics that are not (yet) needed for the IB CS exam, like the **switch** structure and the use of command line parameters. I hope that in this way I have reinforced all the material presented in my Foundations of Java Programming. Another thing that makes this textbook different is that you will notice some repetition. Some important keywords and computer science concepts are presented several times, because the final goal is not just learning how to program in Java, but also getting good marks on the IB CS exam. The students need to see the important material often. Only through repetition the computer science topics will be retained, and the technical vocabulary and the algorithms will stick into their (your) long term memory.

Last but not least, I would like to express my gratitude to all the people who have filled the Internet with very useful information about computer science and the Java programming language, including the comics. Many thanks to the websites with free online Java compilers, and to Oracle and NetBeans.

Even though I went through several revisions of this typed material, I am sure that these class notes can still be improved. If you find any typos, errors, bugs, or if you have any useful suggestions, please email me at cgaleriu@yahoo.com .

Thank you,

Călin Galeriu

# 1. Three options for running the HelloWorld Java program

There are three possible ways to type, compile, and execute a Java program.

You may use an online Java compiler. This is the best option for very short programs. Be aware that, because of security concerns, Java programs executed by an online compiler will not be able to read from and write into text files on your computer's hard drive.

You may use an Integrated Development Environment (IDE). Two very popular options are the NetBeans IDE and the Eclipse IDE. Your Java programming will not come to a halt whenever the Internet connection is down. The IDE option is preferred for longer Java programs, which are written as stand-alone applications. Remember that you will have to write such a long and complex Java program for your IB CS Internal Assessment component.

You may also use a Command Line Interface (CLI) programming environment. This option avoids the Graphical User Interface (GUI) of the friendlier IDE, and is very seldom used. The **javac.exe** compiler and the **java.exe** interpreter are needed for Java programs that use command line parameters.

## 1.1. The online Java compiler option

Step 1. Launch your trusted Internet browser and then go to:

**https://www.onlinegdb.com/**

Back-up plan: If the above web site is not working then to go to:

**https://www.jdoodle.com/online-java-compiler/**

Step 2. From the drop-down Language menu, in the upper right corner of the web page, select **Java** . The **HelloWorld** Java program will automatically shows up.

---

The online compiler at **www.onlinegdb.com** does not use a package name, all the Java source files are automatically made part of the same package. The name of the first Java source file is **Main.java** , and the name of the public class in this file is **Main** . These two names cannot be changed to something else.

---

Step 3. Delete all the comments that were automatically included in the Java program, and align the curly braces on the left side. The **HelloWorld** Java program should look like this:

```
Main.java
1    public class Main
2    {
3        public static void main(String[] args)
4        {
5            System.out.println("Hello World");
6        }
7    }
8
```

Step 4. Click on the green **Run** button.

 Run

**1.2. Installing the NetBeans Java Integrated Development Environment**

When you are downloading and installing the NetBeans Integrated Development Environment (IDE) you are also downloading and installing the Java Development Kit (JDK) with Java 8.

Step 1. Go to:

**https://www.oracle.com/technetwork/java/javase/downloads/jdk-netbeans-jsp-3413139-esa.html**

Step 2. Check the Accept License Agreement option.

Step 3. Click on the appropriate download link. For a not too old PC running the Windows operating system, the file to download is **jdk-8u111-nb-8_2-windows-x64.exe** .

**Warning!** You need to have PC administrator rights in order to move forward with the installation process.

Step 4. Click on the downloaded file.

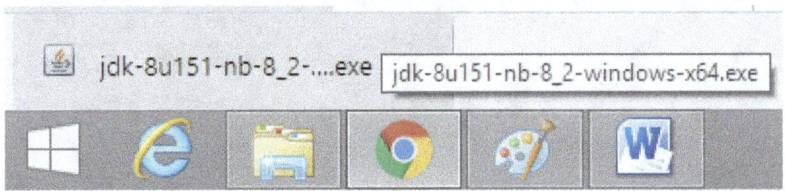

Step 5. Click on the **Next** button three times, then click on the **Install** button.

Step 6. Uncheck the box that says "Contribute to the NetBeans project by providing anonymous usage data" and then click on the **Finish** button.

Step 7. Double click on the NetBeans shortcut link on the desktop whenever you want to launch the NetBeans Integrated Development Environment (IDE).

**1.3. The NetBeans Java Integrated Development Environment option**

After downloading and installing the NetBeans IDE, you are ready to type, compile, and execute the **HelloWorld** Java program in this programming environment.

Step 1. Double click on the NetBeans shortcut link on the desktop.

Step 2. From the menu select **File|New Project...** or click on the **New Project** button.

Step 3. In the **New Project** window the **Java Application** option should be already selected. Click on the **Next** button.

Step 4. In the **New Java Application** window type the **HelloWorld** project name. The **Create Main Class** checkbox should be checked. Click on the **Finish** button.

The **HelloWorld** project name was used by NetBeans in three different places. The name of the newly created Java source file is **HelloWorld.java** , the name of the related Java package is **helloworld** , and the name of the related Java class is **HelloWorld** .

Step 5. Delete all the comments that were automatically included in the Java program, and align the curly braces on the left side.

In Java, anything that follows the double forward slash // , all the way to the end of the line, is a comment . Multi-line comments can be added between the /* and */ marks. Special /** marks are used for Javadoc comments. Javadoc comments are not needed for the IB CS exam.

Step 6. Type the line:   System.out.println("Hello World!");

The program should look like this:

```
1    package helloworld;
2    public class HelloWorld
3    {
4        public static void main(String[] args)
5        {
6            System.out.println("Hello World!");
7        }
8    }
```

Step 7. Click on the **Save All** button.

Step 8. Click on the **Run Project** button.

## 1.4. The Command Line Interface option ( javac.exe and java.exe )

Step 1. Go to the root of your hard disk (**C:\**) and create a new folder. Right-click with the mouse, then select **New|Folder** . Change the name of the folder from **New folder** to **JavaPrograms** .

Step 2. Inside the **JavaPrograms** folder create a new text file. Right-click with the mouse, then select **New|Text Document** . Change the name of the text file from **New Text Document.txt** to **HelloWorld.java** . The computer will give you a warning message that you should ignore.

**Warning!** Sometimes you cannot see the file name extension, and as a result you cannot change it from **.txt** to **.java** . To make the file name extension visible you should search for **Folder Options** (in Windows 8) or **File Explorer Options** (in Windows 10), and then uncheck the **Hide extensions for files of known type** check box.

Step 3. Using **Notepad**, open the **HelloWorld.java** source file, type the Java program as shown below, and then save the text file and close Notepad. The **HelloWorld.java** source file should look like this:

```
HelloWorld.java - Notepad
File  Edit  Format  View  Help

public class HelloWorld
{
    public static void main(String[] args)
    {
        System.out.println("Hello World!");
    }
}
```

Step 4. Open a Command Prompt window. Search for Command Prompt if you need to find it.

Step 5a. Type **cd C:\JavaPrograms**<ENTER>. This will move the command prompt to the **JavaPrograms** directory (folder), which becomes the current directory.

Step 5b. Type **dir**<ENTER>. This will show all the files and folders in the current directory. You should have the **HelloWorld.java** Java source file there.

Step 5c. Type **set path=C:\Program Files\Java\jdk1.8.0_111\bin**<ENTER> with no extra spaces. This will tell the computer where to find the **javac.exe** and the **java.exe** executable files.

| |
|---|
| **Warning!** If you have a different version of the Java Development Kit (JDK) installed, then you will have to modify the numbers in the above path accordingly. |

Step 5d. Type **javac HelloWorld.java**<ENTER>. The **javac.exe** compiler will compile the Java source file into **Bytecode language**, and then it will save the compiled output into **HelloWorld.class** , a Java **.class** file. At this step some students get confused because "nothing happens". Be happy if the computer doesn't print anything now, because this means that there is no error message!

Step 5e. Type **dir**<ENTER>. Verify that the **HelloWorld.class** file is indeed there.

Step 5f. Type **java HelloWorld**<ENTER>. The **java.exe** interpreter (the Java Virtual Machine) will turn the Bytecode into **machine code**, and then the machine code will get executed, one instruction at a time. The machine code is specific to the computer that runs the program, but since the Bytecode language is very close to the actual machine code language, the **java.exe** interpreter is super-fast.

A successful compilation and execution of the **HelloWorld** Java program looks like this:

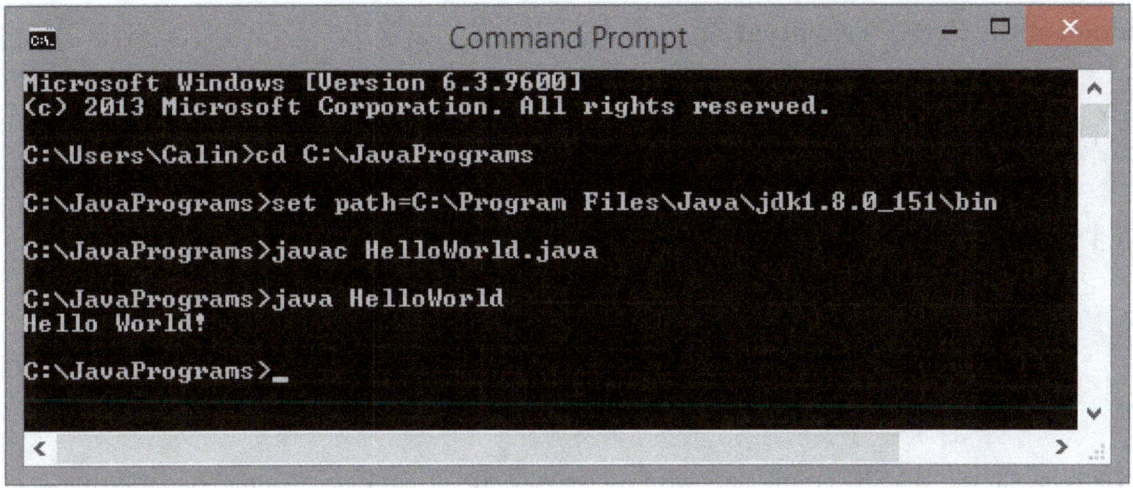

## 2. Why does the simplest Java program look so complicated?

The **HelloWorld** program is, traditionally, the first program that someone new to computer programming learns. This is the simplest program in any programming language. This short computer program is meant to decrease anxiety, build self-confidence, and give the students a good start on a smooth learning path. But why does this **HelloWorld** , the simplest Java program, look so complicated? The answer to this question is related to the historical evolution of computer programming languages.

### 2.1. The BASIC version of the HelloWorld program

The BASIC version of the **HelloWorld** program looks like this:

```
10 PRINT "Hello World!"
```

A BASIC program consists of a sequence of numbered instruction lines. The **entry point** of a computer program is the first instruction that gets  executed. The entry point of a BASIC program is either the first line of that program, or the line number specified after the RUN command (when it is given).

### 2.2. The C version of the HelloWorld program

The C version of the **HelloWorld** program looks like this:

```
#include <stdio.h>
void main()
{
        printf("Hello World!");
}
```

Instead of **PRINT** , a simple BASIC command, we now have **printf()** , a C function. The first line tells the C compiler that the **printf()** function will be found in the **stdio** library. Presumably we could find a different **printf()** function in a different library. This was not an option in BASIC, where **PRINT** is a keyword, and where the printing of text is automatically done on the PC monitor.

A semicolon **;** character is needed at the end of the **printf()** instruction.

A C program consists of a series of declarations and definitions of variables and functions, and also the instructions that use these variables and functions. C programs don't have line numbers, that was a good idea only when computer programs were not very long. The entry point of a C program is the **main()** function.

In our simple C program the **main()** function does not return any value, therefore its output is of type **void** . This is not always the case, in general the **main()** function can return an integer number of type **int** , which then can be used by the operating system as an error code.

## 2.3. The Java version of the HelloWorld program

The Java version of the **HelloWorld** program looks like this:

```
// Java Example 1
public class Main
{
        public static void main(String[] args)
        {
                System.out.println("Hello World!");
        }
}
```

The first line, which starts with a double forward slash, is just a comment line. In Java anything from a double forward slash // until the end on the line is a comment.

In contrast to the C program above, the **main()** function of the Java program is now nested inside another structure, the definition of the **public class Main** . This is because in Java everything must be part of a class. A Java class is a template for Java objects, the same way a cookie cutter is a template for cookies. A Java object is a data structure that may contain variables, functions, or other objects. The class of an object is like the variable type of a variable. The class definition describes what variables (also called fields, attributes, or properties), functions (also called methods), or other objects an object of that given class may have. In our example the **Main** class has only one function, the function named **main()** . The entry point of a Java program is the **main()** function.

We notice that the **main()** function has an input argument, **String[] args** , which stands for an array of **String** objects. **String** objects are used by Java programs to handle text strings. The **HelloWorld** C program could also be written with input arguments, just like the Java program, but since the input arguments (the command line parameters) are never used by our **HelloWorld** program, that would be an unnecessary complication. In Java we have to include the input arguments, regardless of whether we use them or not. Java programs with command line parameters are discussed in Chapter 14.

The keyword **public** means that the **Main** class and the **main()** function can be seen from anywhere in the program. The keyword **static** means that there is only one copy of the **main()** function, existing in Random Access Memory (RAM) without the need to create an object of class **Main** .

A semicolon **;** character is needed at the end of the **System.out.println()** instruction. A semicolon is needed after every Java program instruction.

**System.out** is a Java object that manages the output of alphanumeric characters on the PC monitor, and **println()** is a function (a method) of the **System.out** object, used for printing alphanumeric text one line at a time.

> In summary, the Java program needs a **main()** function because this is the entry point of the program. In Java the **main()** function can exist only as a **public static** method of a **public** class. The Java **main()** function has to declare the input arguments (the command line parameters) **String[] args** regardless of whether these input arguments are used by the Java program or not.

## 3. Variables: primitive variable types, text strings, and constants

Remember that in mathematics a variable **x** is a placeholder for a number. The number **x** may be an unknown, like for example in the equation **2x + 3 = 5** , or the number **x** may take different values, like for example in the slope-intercept equation of a straight line **y = 2x + 3** .

In computer programming variables work in the same way. Inside a computer the content (the value) of a variable is stored in **Random Access Memory** (RAM), occupying a given amount of space at a given memory address. In general a variable has:

- A name (the name of a storage location), for example **x** .
- A type, for example **int**, when the variable is a signed integer number .
- A value (the content of the storage location), for example **505** .
- An address in RAM. In Java we do not have direct access to this information.
- A size in RAM. In Java a variable of type **int** is stored in RAM using 4 bytes = 32 bits.
- A scope. The variable exists, while the program is running, only in a part of the code.

**Warning!** In Java a variable exists only between the nearest set of closed curly braces { } that contain the declaration of that variable.

A **declaration statement** gives the type of a variable. For example:   int x;

An **assignment statement** gives the value of a variable. For example:   x = 505;

In general the declaration of the type of a variable must be done before the assignment of a value to that variable.

An **initialization statement** brings together the declaration of a variable and the initial assignment of a value. For example:   int x = 505;

Java has 8 **primitive variable types**. We call them primitive because they come as a standard feature of the Java language, to distinguish them from **user defined variable types**. The name, size in RAM, and range of each of these 8 primitive variable types are listed below.

---

**byte** = 8-bit signed integer, −128 ... 127

**short** = 16-bit signed integer, −32,768 ... 32,767

**int** = 32-bit signed integer, −2,147,483,648 ... 2,147,483,647

**long** = 64-bit signed integer, −9,223,372,036,854,775,808 ... 9,223,372,036,854,775,807

**float** = 32-bit single precision floating point number,

$$\pm 3.40282347 \times 10^{38} \ ... \ \pm 1.40239846 \times 10^{-45}$$

**double** = 64-bit double precision floating point number,

$$\pm 1.7976931348623157 \times 10^{308} \ ... \ \pm 4.9406564584124654 \times 10^{-324}$$

**char** = 16-bit Unicode character, 0 ... 65,535

**boolean** = **true** or **false**

---

Variables of type **short** and **float** are not required for the IB Computer Science exam.

Numerical values of type **long** have to end in **L** or **l** , and numerical values of type **float** have to end in **F** or **f** . Numerical values of type **double** may end in **D** or **d** , this rule is optional. Numbers in scientific notation are written using **E** or **e**, which stands for a power of 10. For example 3.4E5 stands for $3.4 \times 10^5$.

Characters can be entered between single quotes ('a'), using the Unicode value in hexadecimal form ('\u0066'), or as a **special escape sequence** ('\b' = backspace, '\n' = newline, '\t' = tab, '\r' = carriage return, '\f' = form feed, '\\' = backslash, '\'' = single quote, '\"' = double quote).

The next program, Java Example 2, demonstrates the use of all the Java primitive variable types.

```
// Java Example 2
public class Main
{
        public static void main(String[] args)
        {
                byte b = 100;
                System.out.println("b = " + b);
                short i = 3000;
                System.out.println("i = " + i);
                int j = 40000;
                System.out.println("j = " + j);
                long k = 5000000000L;
                System.out.println("k = " + k);
                float x = 3.1416F;
                System.out.println("x = " + x);
                double y = 7.8E200;
                System.out.println("y = " + y);
                char c = 'a';
                System.out.println("c = " + c);
                boolean a = true;
                System.out.println("a = " + a);
        }
}
```

The Java programming language, unlike more powerful programming languages like C and C++, does not have user defined variable types. For this reason, for example, Java is not a good choice when we need to perform intensive computations involving complex (imaginary) numbers.

In Java text strings are not variables, but objects of type **String**. Think of an **object** of type **String** as a **primitive variable** of type text string packaged together with some **functions** that act on text strings.

**A historical note:** Objects have become an important part of the C++ programming language when the Windows operating system has replaced MS DOS. All the windows of the applications running under Windows are objects. These **objects** share the same kind of **primitive variables** (for example, the x and y pixel coordinates of the corners of the rectangular shape) and the same kind of **functions** (for example, what to do when the user clicks with the mouse on the Minimize, Restore, and Close buttons.

However, because text strings are used very often, in Java the declaration, assignment, and initialization of **String** objects is simplified, and it looks just like the declaration, assignment, and initialization of primitive variables. In a text string the information is entered between double quotation marks.

Please also notice that in Java the plus symbol can be used as a concatenation operator for **String** objects, merging (combining, adding) two or more text strings together into just one text string. Example: "abc" + "def" = "abcdef"

The next program, Java Example 3, shows how to print "Hello World!" using text strings.

```
// Java Example 3
public class Main
{
        public static void main(String[] args)
        {
                String word1;   // a declaration statement
                word1 = "Hello";   // an assignment statement
                String word2 = "World";   // an initialization statement
                System.out.println(word1 + " " + word2 + "!");
        }
}
```

A variable in a computer program that is assigned a value only once, being initialized at compile time, is called a **constant**. In Java constants are declared using the **final** keyword. This will prevent an accidental change of the value of the constant. Most often the **static** keyword is also used, to make the constant available inside the program even without an instantiated (created) object.

**Warning!** Please note that in Java a **static** function, like the **static void main()** function, can only access **static** methods, variables, or constants from the outside of the respective function.

The next program, Java Example 4, uses an **int** constant named **SOS** that has a value of 505 .

```
// Java Example 4
public class Main
{
        static final int SOS = 505;

        public static void main(String[] args)
        {
                System.out.println("SOS = " + SOS);
        }
}
```

Java has some **naming conventions** that you should follow.

The names of variables, methods, and objects are written without underscores, starting with a lower case letter. Separation between more words is done with upper case letters.

Examples: **i** , **age** , **maxSpeed** , **numberOfPeople** , **main()** , **myBook** , **getName()**

The names of classes are written without underscores, starting with an upper case letter. Separation between more words is done with upper case letters.

Examples: **String** , **Random** , **Book** , **ImageSprite** , **ChessBoard**

The names of constants are written with underscores, using only upper case letters.

Examples: **X** , **LENGTH** , **MAX_HEIGHT** , **NUMBER_OF_PIXELS**

# 4. Data input from the keyboard with the Scanner and IBIO classes

You have learned that a Java program can output data (to the computer monitor) using the **System.out.println()** method. But how can a Java program input data (from the computer keyboard)? One way to do this is with the help of the **Scanner** class.

The next program, Java Example 5, is similar to Java Example 2, but this time all the values of the primitive variables are read from the keyboard, instead of being given inside the code.

```java
// Java Example 5
import java.util.Scanner;
public class Main
{
        public static void main(String[] args)
        {
                Scanner kbdInput = new Scanner(System.in);
                System.out.print("byte b = ? ");   // input : 100
                byte b = kbdInput.nextByte();
                System.out.println("b = " + b);
                System.out.print("short i = ? ");   // input : 3000
                short i = kbdInput.nextShort();
                System.out.println("i = " + i);
                System.out.print("int j = ? ");   // input : 40000
                int j = kbdInput.nextInt();
                System.out.println("j = " + j);
                System.out.print("long k = ? ");   // input : 5000000000
                long k = kbdInput.nextLong();
                System.out.println("k = " + k);
                System.out.print("float x = ? ");   // input : 3.1416
                float x = kbdInput.nextFloat();
                System.out.println("x = " + x);
                System.out.print("double y = ? ");   // input : 7.8E200
                double y = kbdInput.nextDouble();
                System.out.println("y = " + y);
                System.out.print("char c = ? ");   // input : a
                char c = kbdInput.next().charAt(0);
                System.out.println("c = " + c);
                System.out.print("boolean a = ? ");   // input : true
                boolean a = kbdInput.nextBoolean();
                System.out.println("a = " + a);
        }
}
```

One important thing to notice is the   import java.util.Scanner;   line, which tells the Java compiler to look for the definition and the implementation of the **Scanner** class in the **java.util** package.

Another thing to notice is the   Scanner kbdInput = new Scanner(System.in);   line. Here **kbdInput** is the name of an object of type (of class) **Scanner** . The first part of the line holds the declaration of the **kbdInput** object of class **Scanner** . The second part of the line holds the creation (the instantiation) of the **kbdInput** object, which is done with the help of the **new** keyword and the **Scanner(System.in)** method (function) . The **Scanner()** function, with the same name as the **Scanner** class, is called the constructor of this class. **System.in** is an input parameter, a Java object that identifies the computer keyboard as the source of the alphanumeric stream of data.

Once the **kbdInput** object is created (and therefore exists in RAM), we can use some of its methods to input data. The program demonstrates the use of the **nextByte()** , **nextShort()** , **nextInt()** , **nextLong()** , **nextFloat()** , **nextDouble()** , **next()** , and **nextBoolean()** methods, which return variables of type **byte** , **short** , **int** , **long** , **float** , **double** , an object of type **String** , and a variable of type **boolean** . Please notice how **kbdInput** , the name of the object, shows up in front of each method, and how the two are connected by a dot. The object returned by the **kbdInput.next()** function is of type **String** , and the **charAt(0)** method of the **String** class selects the first alphanumeric character of a given text string. This character is what the **kbdInput.next().charAt(0)** expression returns as a value.

What happens if instead of typing 100<ENTER> you type 100 3000<ENTER> ? This shows that everything you type on the computer keyboard is saved in a buffer, which is a dedicated memory space. This keyboard input buffer is then checked by the methods of the **Scanner** class.

What happens if instead of typing 100<ENTER> you type z<ENTER> ? There are ways to prevent the program from crashing due to invalid input. The **Scanner** class has methods that verify the type of the alphanumeric input received. Nonetheless, in order to keep the Java programs short and simple, we will assume that the users know what they are supposed to do, and that they always input some valid information.

The next program, Java Example 6, uses the **Scanner** class to read a text string (a word) from the keyboard. The word consists of all the alphanumeric characters that show up in the typed text string before the special delimiter character (usually the empty space character) or before the end of the text string, signaled by <ENTER> . The program demonstrates the use of the **next()** method, which returns an object of type **String** .

```
// Java Example 6
import java.util.Scanner;
public class Main
{
        public static void main(String[] args)
        {
                Scanner kbdInput = new Scanner(System.in);
                System.out.print("String word = ? ");   // input : Happy New Year!
                String word = kbdInput.next();
                System.out.println("word = " + word);   // output : Happy
        }
}
```

What happens if you try to enter an empty text string, or an empty space?

The next program, Java Example 7, uses the **Scanner** class to read a text string (a sentence) from the keyboard. The sentence consists of all the alphanumeric characters that show up in the typed text string before the end of the text string, signaled by <ENTER>. The program demonstrates the use of the **nextLine()** method, which returns an object of type **String** .

```java
// Java Example 7
import java.util.Scanner;
public class Main
{
        public static void main(String[] args)
        {
                Scanner kbdInput = new Scanner(System.in);
                System.out.print("String sentence = ? ");   // input : Happy Chinese New Year!
                String sentence = kbdInput.nextLine();
                System.out.println("sentence = " + sentence);   // output : Happy Chinese New Year!
        }
}
```

What happens if you try to enter an empty text string, or an empty space?

There is an alternative to the **Scanner** class, this is the **IBIO** class. The **IBIO** class was created by the International Baccalaureate computer science experts in order to assist with data input and output operations. The next program, Java Example 8, shows how to use the IBIO class.

Go to  **https://www.onlinegdb.com/** . Start the online Java compiler, and click on the **New File** button. Give the new file the name **IBIO.java** . Copy and paste inside the new file all the content of the **IBIO.java** file, which you may find at
**https://stackoverflow.com/questions/29000103/java-code-for-guessing-game-not-printing-anything**

```java
// Java Example 8
public class Main
{
        public static void main(String[] args)
        {
                byte b = IBIO.inputByte("byte b = ? ");   // input : 100
                IBIO.output("b = " + b);
                int j = IBIO.inputInt("int j = ? ");   // input : 40000
                IBIO.output("j = " + j);
                long k = IBIO.inputLong("long k = ? ");   // input : 5000000000
                IBIO.output("k = " + k);
                double y = IBIO.inputDouble("double y = ? ");   // input : 7.8E200
                IBIO.output("y = " + y);
                char c = IBIO.inputChar("char c = ? ");   // input : a
                IBIO.output("c = " + c);
                boolean a = IBIO.inputBoolean("boolean a = ? ");   // input : true
                IBIO.output("a = " + a);
                String word = IBIO.inputString("String word = ? ");   // input : Happy
                IBIO.output("word = " + word);
        }
}
```

# 5. Operators: arithmetic, relational, and logical

## 5.1. The Java arithmetic operators

The Java **arithmetic operators** have numbers as input and numbers as output.

| The Java arithmetic operators are  + , − , * , / , % , ++ , — . |
|---|

+ (addition)   Example: 13 + 5 = 18

– (subtraction)   Example: 13 – 5 = 8

* (multiplication)   Example: 13 * 5 = 65

/ (division)   Example: 13.0 / 5.0 = 2.6

/ (integer division)   Example: 13 / 5 = 2        This is the quotient of an integer division.

% (modulus)   Example: 13 % 5 = 3        This is the remainder of an integer division.

++ (increment)   Example: 13++ = 14

— (decrement)   Example: 5— = 4

---

**Warning!** It is very easy to make mistakes because x++ (post-increment) is not the same as ++x (pre-increment), and x— (post-decrement) is not the same as —x (pre-decrement).

y = x++;  means  { y = x; x = x + 1; } , while  y = ++x  means  { x = x + 1; y = x; } .

y = x—;  means  { y = x; x = x – 1; } , while  y = —x  means  { x = x – 1; y = x; } .

---

IB CS requirement: Use  **x = x + 1**  instead of  **x++**  or  **++x** , and  **x = x – 1**  instead of  **x—**  or  **—x** .

The next program, Java Example 9, demonstrates how to do some simple arithmetic calculations.

```
// Java Example 9
public class Main
{
        public static void main(String[] args)
        {
                int i = 13;
                int j = 5;
                double x = 13.0;
                double y = 5.0;
                System.out.println(i + j);   // output : 18
                System.out.println(i - j);   // output : 8
                System.out.println(i * j);   // output : 65
                System.out.println(x / y);   // output : 2.6
                System.out.println(i / j);   // output : 2
                System.out.println(i % j);   // output : 3
                System.out.println(i / y);   // output : 2.6

        }

}
```

## 5.2. The Java relational operators

The Java **relational operators** have numbers as input and boolean values as output.

> The Java relational operators are  == , != , < , > , <= , >= .

== (is equal to)   Example: 13 == 5 is **false** .

!= (is not equal to)   Example: 13 != 5 is **true** .

< (is less than)   Example: 13 < 5 is **false** .

> (is greater than)   Example: 13 > 5 is **true** .

<= (is less than or equal to)   Example: 13 <= 5 is **false** .

>= (is greater than or equal to)   Example: 13 >= 5 is **true** .

The Java relational operators return a result (of type **boolean**) that can only be **true** or **false**.

> **Warning!** Be careful when you read out loud expressions with relational operators. "Five is less than thirteen" means 5 < 13, but "five less than thirteen" means 13 − 5.

The next program, Java Example 10, evaluates some **boolean expressions** (logical statements that can only be **true** or **false**) that use relational operators.

```
// Java Example 10
public class Main
{
        public static void main(String[] args)
        {
                int i = 13;
                int j = 5;
                System.out.println(i == j);   // output : false
                System.out.println(i != j);   // output : true
                System.out.println(i < j);   // output : false
                System.out.println(i > j);   // output : true
                System.out.println(i <= j);   // output : false
                System.out.println(i >= j);   // output : true
        }
}
```

## 5.3. The Java logical operators

The Java **logical operators** have boolean values as input and boolean values as output.

> The Java logical operators are  && , || , ! .

&& (AND)  Example:  (13 < 5) && (13 > 5) is **false**    because    **false** AND **true** is **false** .

|| (OR)  Example:  (13 < 5) || (13 > 5) is **true**    because    **false** OR **true** is **true** .

! (NOT)  Example:  !(13 < 5) is **true**    because    NOT **false** is **true** .

The Java logical operators return a result (of type **boolean**) that can only be **true** or **false**.

> **Warning!** It is important to realize that the logical operators, just like the arithmetic operators, are evaluated according to a predetermined order of operations: NOT is evaluated first, AND is evaluated next, and OR is evaluated last.

Since using the order of operations for logical operators is not something very intuitive to humans, it is good programming practice to use parentheses in order to clarify the meaning of more complex boolean expressions. For example,

write  **X = [(NOT A) AND B] OR [A AND (NOT B)]**   (in Java:  x = ((!A) && B) || (A && (!B));  )

instead of  **X = NOT A AND B OR A AND NOT B**   (in Java:  x = !A && B || A && !B;  )

even though, from the computer's perspective, it is the same thing.

The next program, Java Example 11, evaluates some simple boolean expressions (logical statements that can only be **true** or **false**) that use logical operators.

```java
// Java Example 11
public class Main
{
        public static void main(String[] args)
        {
           boolean a = false;
           boolean b = true;
           System.out.println(a && b);   // output : false
           System.out.println(a || b);   // output : true
           System.out.println(!a);   // output : true
        }
}
```

The input-output tables below give the boolean values of all the simple boolean expressions with logical operators. These tables have to be memorized. One way to memorize these tables is to think of **false** as 0, to think of **true** as 1 (or 2), to think of AND as multiplication, and to think of OR as addition.

| X | Y | X AND Y |
|---|---|---------|
| false | false | false |
| false | true | false |
| true | false | false |
| true | true | true |

| X | Y | X OR Y |
|---|---|--------|
| false | false | false |
| false | true | true |
| true | false | true |
| true | true | true |

| X | NOT X |
|---|-------|
| false | true |
| true | false |

Java has more operators (bitwise operators, assignment operators, etc.) but they are not required for the IB Computer Science exam. For a list of all the Java operators and their order of operations, please go to: **https://introcs.cs.princeton.edu/java/11precedence/**

# 6. Control flow: conditional statements

All the Java programs given as examples until now (Java examples from 1 to 11) have a very simple structure. During execution the program starts at the first instruction line of the **main()** function, and then executes in a sequence all the instruction lines of the **main()** function. After executing the last instruction line of the **main()** function, the program stops. Most computer programs need more flexibility, they need to execute or skip different segments of code depending on various conditions. To implement such a behavior the Java language has the **if** , **else** , **switch** , and **break** keywords.

For simplicity, the conditions tested in the next Java examples will be based on random numbers. We will use   int i = (int) (6*Math.random() + 1);   to simulate the roll of a die. This is an integer expression that returns 1, 2, 3, 4, 5, or 6. There is more information about random numbers in Chapter 16.

## 6.1. The IF structure

The simplest **if** structure is this:

**if (conditionA) instructionA;**

The **instructionA** instruction will be executed only when the **conditionA** condition is **true** . Otherwise the program simply goes to the next instruction after the **if** structure. Although not mandatory, the **instructionA** instruction could be placed inside curly braces. This is good programming practice, helping the readability and the future maintenance of your code.

**if (conditionA) { instructionA; }**

The curly braces become mandatory when more than one instruction have to be executed, as a block of instructions, when the **conditionA** condition is **true**.

**if (conditionA) { instructionA1; instructionA2; instructionA3; }**

The flowchart of the **if** structure is this:

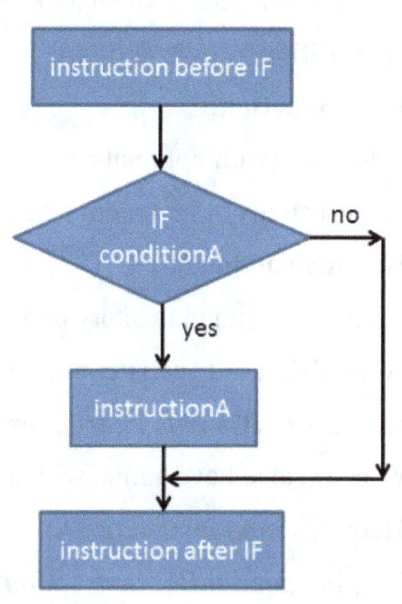

The next program, Java Example 12, prints "WINNER!" whenever the integer random number **i** happens to be 6. The program doesn't print "WINNER!" otherwise. Please notice that the round brackets **( )** around the **i == 6** tested condition are mandatory.

```java
// Java Example 12
public class Main
{
        public static void main(String[] args)
        {
                int i = (int) (6*Math.random() + 1);   // roll of the die
                System.out.println("i = " + i);   // the statement before IF
                if (i == 6)
                {
                        System.out.println("WINNER!");
                }
                System.out.println("i = " + i);   // the statement after IF
        }
}
```

## 6.2. The IF-ELSE structure

What do we do when the program is supposed to do something when the tested condition is **true** , and something else when the tested condition is **false** ? We could write something like this:

**if (conditionA) instructionA;**

**if (NOT conditionA) instructionB;**

but that would be wasteful, since the same condition is tested twice. We know that **NOT conditionA** is **false** when **conditionA** is **true**, and we know that **NOT conditionA** is **true** when **conditionA** is **false** .

To avoid this waste of computing resources, and to test the **boolean** condition only once, we implement the **if-else** structure, which looks like this:

**if (conditionA) instructionA;**

**else instructionB;**

or like this (with optional curly braces for single instructions):

**if (conditionA) { instructionA; }**

**else { instructionB; }**

or like this (with mandatory curly braces for blocks of instructions):

**if (conditionA) { instructionA1; instructionA2; instructionA3; }**

**else { instructionB1; instructionB2; instructionB3; }**

We could also have a mix, with a single instruction paired up with a block of instructions, like this:

**if (conditionA) instructionA;**

**else { instructionB1; instructionB2; instructionB3; }**

or with a block of instructions paired up with a single instruction, like this:

**if (conditionA) { instructionA1; instructionA2; instructionA3; }**

**else instructionB;**

The flowchart of the **if-else** structure is this:

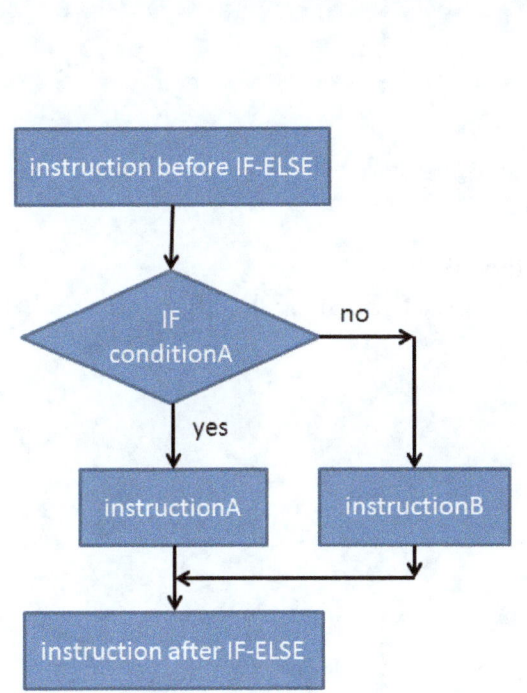

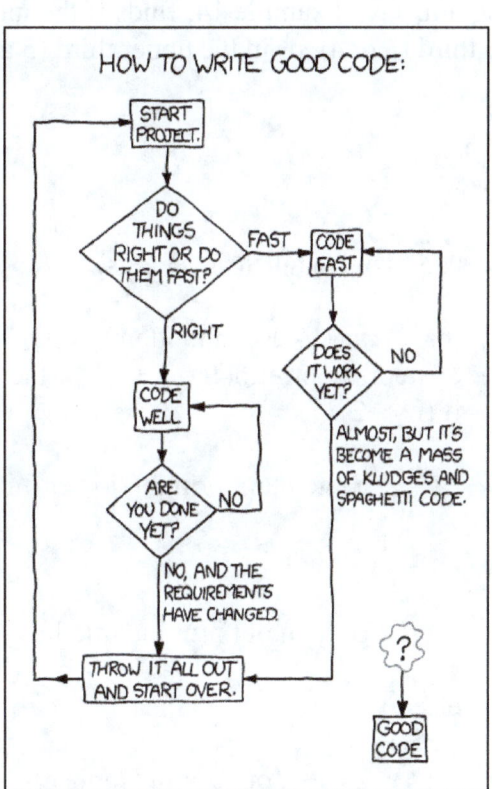

The next program, Java Example 13, finds if the integer random number **i** is odd or even, and then prints this information. When is a number even? When the remainder of an integer division by 2 is 0.

```java
// Java Example 13
public class Main
{
        public static void main(String[] args)
        {
                int i = (int) (6*Math.random() + 1);   // roll of the die
                System.out.println("i = " + i);   // the statement before IF-ELSE
                if (i%2 == 0)
                {
                        System.out.println("even number");
                }
                else
                {
                        System.out.println("odd number");
                }
                System.out.println("i = " + i);   // the statement after IF-ELSE
        }
}
```

More complex situations, when there are more than 2 possible outcomes, require more complex **if** structures. Please notice that in the above flowcharts the two instruction blocks **instructionA** and **instructionB** can themselves be made from other **if** or **if-else** structures.

The next program, Java Example 14, finds if the integer random number **i** is in the lower third (1 or 2), in the middle third (3 or 4), or in the upper third (5 and 6), and then prints this information.

```java
// Java Example 14
public class Main
{
        public static void main(String[] args)
        {
                int i = (int) (6*Math.random() + 1);   // roll of the die
                System.out.println("i = " + i);   // the statement before IF-ELSE-IF-ELSE
                if (i <= 2)
                {
                        System.out.println("lower third");
                }
                else if (i <= 4)
                {
                        System.out.println("middle third");
                }
                else
                {
                        System.out.println("upper third");
                }
                System.out.println("i = " + i);   // the statement after IF-ELSE-IF-ELSE
        }
}
```

Notice that the **if-else-if-else** structure used above is very efficient. Only two inequalities are tested by the program. A less efficient alternative is to use three simple **if** structures, but then four inequalities are tested, as shown below.

```java
if (i <= 2) System.out.println("lower third");

if (i > 2 && i < 5) System.out.println("middle third");

if (i >= 5) System.out.println("upper third");
```

As expected, two of these four inequalities are not independent, since **!(i <= 2)** is the same as **i > 2** , and **!(i >= 5)** is the same as **i < 5** .

What do we do if we want the program to spell in words the value of the random number? We could use six simple **if** statements, as shown below:

```java
if (i == 1) System.out.println("one");

if (i == 2) System.out.println("two");

if (i == 3) System.out.println("three");

if (i == 4) System.out.println("four");
```

```
if (i == 5) System.out.println("five");
```

```
if (i == 6) System.out.println("six");
```

This program is very inefficient because it will test all six equalities every time, for any integer random number **i** . Often the testing will continue even after the correct message has been printed. This is wasteful, because another **true** condition will never be found again. A better option is to use a very long **if-else-if-else-if-else-if-else-if-else** structure, as shown below:

```
if (i == 1) System.out.println("one");
```

```
else if (i == 2) System.out.println("two");
```

```
else if (i == 3) System.out.println("three");
```

```
else if (i == 4) System.out.println("four");
```

```
else if (i == 5) System.out.println("five");
```

```
else System.out.println("six");
```

The above program is more efficient. Once a match is found, the message is printed and the remaining equalities are no longer checked. Also, there is no need to check for **i == 6** , because at this point in the program there is no other available option for the value of the integer random number **i** .

## 6.3. The SWITCH structure

Another option is to use a **switch(i)** statement, as shown in Java Example 15.

```
// Java Example 15
public class Main
{
        public static void main(String[] args)
        {
                int i = (int) (6*Math.random() + 1);   // roll of the die
                System.out.println("i = " + i);   // the statement before SWITCH
                switch(i)
                {
                        case 1 : System.out.println("one");
                                break;
                        case 2 : System.out.println("two");
                                break;
                        case 3 : System.out.println("three");
                                break;
                        case 4 : System.out.println("four");
                                break;
                        case 5 : System.out.println("five");
                                break;
                        default : System.out.println("six");
                }
                System.out.println("i = " + i);   // the statement after SWITCH
        }
}
```

The **switch(i)** instruction works like a **go to case i** instruction, available in other programming languages. There is no **go to** instruction in Java.

The **default** case is executed when no good match is found. The **default** case is optional. In our Java program we could replace the **default** case with case 6 : System.out.println("six"); and the program would perform exactly in the same way.

The **break** statements force the program to exit the **switch** structure, and in this way the computer will continue with the next instruction after the **switch** structure. The **break** statements are optional, but if they are not included then the program will not exit the **switch** structure until the last case (or the **default** case if present) is executed.

The next program, Java Example 16, shows what happens when there are no **break** statements inside a **switch** structure.

```
// Java Example 16
public class Main
{
        public static void main(String[] args)
        {
                int i = (int) (6*Math.random() + 1);   // roll of the die
                System.out.println("i = " + i);   // the statement before SWITCH
                switch(i)
                {
                        case 1 : System.out.println("one");
                        case 2 : System.out.println("two");
                        case 3 : System.out.println("three");
                        case 4 : System.out.println("four");
                        case 5 : System.out.println("five");
                        case 6 : System.out.println("six");
                }
                System.out.println("i = " + i);   // the statement after SWITCH
        }
}
```

Run the program a few times. Is this the desired behavior, or a programming mistake? Can you draw the correct conclusion if you run the program only once, and the integer random number **i** happens to be 6 ?

# 7. Control flow: loops

The flow of control (the control flow) in a program can be sequential (the computer executes one line of code after another, in a sequence), or based on selection (the computer chooses a path or another, depending on some conditional **if** , **if-else** , or **switch** statements), or based on repetition (the computer repeats the instructions inside a loop of code). The loops of code can be controlled by counters (in the case of **for** loops) or by events (in the case of **while** and **do ... while** loops). To implement repetitive structures the Java language has the **for** , **while** , **do**, **continue** , and **break** keywords.

## 7.1. The FOR loop

The structure of a **for** loop is this:

**for(initialize_the_counter ; loop_condition ; change_the_counter) { instructions; }**

The counter is an integer variable that often exists only for the duration of the loop. The **initialize_the_counter** instruction sets the initial value of the counter. When the **loop_condition** becomes **false** the repetition ends, the computer exits the loop, and the next instruction after the **for** loop structure is executed.  The **change_the_counter** instruction is usually an increment (addition of 1) or decrement (subtraction of 1) operation. The **loop_condition** must be related to the value of the counter.

For only one instruction the curly braces are optional, but still recommended as good programming practice. Two or more instructions have to be written inside curly braces. We can also have nested **for** loops, when one of the instructions is itself a **for** loop structure.

The next program, Java Example 17, finds the sum of the integer numbers from 1 to 10. Please notice how the **sum** variable is declared and initialized outside of the **for** loop structure.

```
// Java Example 17
public class Main
{
        public static void main(String[] args)
        {
                int sum = 0;
                for(int i = 1; i <= 10; i = i + 1)
                {
                        System.out.println("i = " + i);
                        sum = sum + i;
                }
                System.out.println("1 + 2 + ... + 10 = " + sum);
        }
}
```

Sometimes the program needs to get out of a loop before the loop condition becomes **false** . Java does not have a **go to** instruction, like the C programming language, but we can use a **break** statement in order to exit the **for** loop and go to the next instruction in the program, the first instruction after the **for** loop structure.

The next program, Java Example 18, finds the sum of the integer numbers from 1 to 6. This program looks exactly like Java Example 17, with one exception: the  if(i == 7) break;  statement forces the program to stop the addition after the first 6 numbers, when the  **i == 7**  condition becomes **true** .

```
// Java Example 18
public class Main
{
        public static void main(String[] args)
        {
                int sum = 0;
                for(int i = 1; i <= 10; i = i + 1)
                {
                        if(i == 7) break;
                        System.out.println("i = " + i);
                        sum = sum + i;
                }
                System.out.println("1 + 2 + ... + 6 = " + sum);
        }
}
```

Another useful instruction is the **continue** statement. This tells the computer to immediately go to the beginning of the **for** loop structure, change the counter, and, in case of a **true** loop condition, proceed with the first instruction in the loop of code.

The next program, Java Example 19, finds the sum of the integer numbers from 1 to 10, skipping 7. This program looks exactly like Java Example 17, with one exception: the  if(i == 7) continue; statement forces the program to skip the addition of number 7.

```
// Java Example 19
public class Main
{
        public static void main(String[] args)
        {
                int sum = 0;
                for(int i = 1; i <= 10; i = i + 1)
                {
                        if(i == 7) continue;
                        System.out.println("i = " + i);
                        sum = sum + i;
                }
                System.out.println("1 + 2 + ... + 10 - 7 = " + sum);
        }
}
```

The next program, Java Example 20, uses nested loops in order to print all the numbers from 0 to 99. The one hundred numbers are printed on ten rows of ten numbers each. For each of the **i** values (in the outer **for** loop) the program executes the instructions for all of the **j** values (in the inner **for** loop). A nested **for** loop structure like this one is often used when working with two-dimensional arrays.

```java
// Java Example 20
public class Main
{
        public static void main(String[] args)
        {
                for(int i = 0; i <= 9; i = i + 1)
                {
                        for(int j = 0; j <= 9; j = j + 1)
                        {
                                System.out.print(i + "" + j + " ");
                        }
                        System.out.println("");   // new line
                }
        }
}
```

## 7.2. The WHILE and the DO...WHILE loops

In some situations we don't know exactly how many times the loop of code has to be repeated. For example, a program reads lines of text from a text file, without knowing how many lines of text the actual text file has. For such situations we can use **while** or **do ... while** loops. The loop condition, for these loops, may or may not be related to a counter.

The structure of a **while** loop is this:

**while(loop_condition) { instructions; }**

The structure of a **do ... while** loop is this:

**do { instructions; } while(loop_condition);**

The **while** loop checks the loop condition before the execution of the code. In some situations the code inside the **while** loop is never executed. The **do .. while** loop checks the loop condition after the execution of the code. The code inside the **do .. while** loop is always executed at least once.

When there is only one instruction inside the loop, the curly braces are optional. Otherwise the curly braces are mandatory. Please notice the semicolon **;** at the end of the **do ... while** structure.

The next program, Java Example 21, finds the sum of the integer numbers from 1 to 10 with the help of a **while** loop.

```java
// Java Example 21
public class Main
{
        public static void main(String[] args)
        {
                int sum = 0;
                int i = 1;  // initialize the counter
                while(i <= 10)   // check the loop condition
                {
                        System.out.println("i = " + i);
                        sum = sum + i;
                        i = i + 1;  // change the counter
                }
                System.out.println("1 + 2 + ... + 10 = " + sum);
        }
}
```

The next program, Java Example 22, finds the sum of the integer numbers from 1 to 10 with the help of a **do ... while** loop.

```java
// Java Example 22
public class Main
{
        public static void main(String[] args)
        {
                int sum = 0;
                int i = 1;  // initialize the counter
                do
                {
                        System.out.println("i = " + i);
                        sum = sum + i;
                        i = i + 1;  // change the counter
                } while(i <= 10);   // check the loop condition
                System.out.println("1 + 2 + ... + 10 = " + sum);
        }
}
```

But beware of the infinite loop! For example, in Java Examples 21 and 22, if the programmer forgets to write the   i = i + 1;   line that changes the counter, the loop condition will always be true, the code inside the loop will be repeated forever, and the program will get stuck in place. As a general rule, inside **while** and **do ... while** loops we must always have a line of code that, eventually, will change the **boolean** value of the loop condition to **false** .

The programmer got stuck in the shower because the instructions on the shampoo bottle said: Lather, Rinse, Repeat.

The next program, Java Example 23, demonstrates a **while** loop without a counter. The program prints integer random numbers, until we get a 6. The last number, the 6, is not printed. Please notice that we have to roll the die inside the **while** loop, but also before it, once.

```java
// Java Example 23
public class Main
{
        public static void main(String[] args)
        {
                int i = (int) (6*Math.random() + 1);   // roll of the die
                while(i != 6)   // check the loop condition
                {
                        System.out.println("i = " + i);
                        i = (int) (6*Math.random() + 1);   // change the value of the loop condition
                }
        }
}
```

The next program, Java Example 24, demonstrates a **do ... while** loop without a counter. The program prints integer random numbers, until we get a 6. The last number, the 6, is also printed.

```java
// Java Example 24
public class Main
{
        public static void main(String[] args)
        {
                int i;
                do
                {
                        i = (int) (6*Math.random() + 1);   // change the value of the loop condition
                        System.out.println("i = " + i);
                } while(i != 6);   // check the loop condition
        }
}
```

## 8. Functions: input and output values, formal and actual parameters

Remember that in mathematics a function **f** is something that has a set of input values (the domain of the function, the set of all possible **x** values), a set of output values (the range of the function, the set of all possible **y** values), and a relationship **y = f(x)** that provides a unique output value **y** for every input value **x**. In computer programming functions work in the same way, with the mention that sometimes a function may not have an input value, or an output value, or both. In Java functions are called methods. The **main()** method used so far has an array of text strings ( **String[] args** ) as the input value, and nothing ( **void** ) as the output value. Notice how, in the declaration of a function, the return type (the variable type of the output value) is written in front of the name of that function, while the names and variable types of the input parameters are written in round brackets after the name of that function.

The next program, Java Example 25, demonstrates how to print "Hello World!" using a function named **printGreeting()** that has no input parameters ( empty round brackets **()** ) and no output value ( **void** ).

```java
// Java Example 25
public class Main
{
        public static void main(String[] args)
        {
                printGreeting();
        }

        static void printGreeting()
        {
                System.out.println("Hello World!");
        }
}
```

The next program, Java Example 26, demonstrates how to print "Hello World!" using a function named **printGreeting()** that has one input parameter ( an object of type **String** ) and no output value ( **void** ).

```java
// Java Example 26
public class Main
{
        public static void main(String[] args)
        {
                String greeting = "Hello World!";
                printGreeting(greeting);
        }

        static void printGreeting(String text)
        {
                System.out.println(text);
        }
}
```

The object named **text** that shows up in the definition of the **printGreeting()** function is called a formal parameter (a formal argument). The object named **greeting** that shows up in the function call of **printGreeting()** is called an actual parameter (an actual argument). During the execution of the **printGreeting()** function, the value of **greeting** (the actual parameter) is assigned to **text** (the formal parameter) inside the body of the **printGreeting()** function. It is possible to give both the formal parameter and the actual parameter the same name, since these two "variables" (text string objects of class **String** ) exist in different places (inside the body of different functions). The **greeting** object (the actual parameter) exists only inside the body of the **main()** function, while the **text** object (the formal parameter) exists only inside the body of the **printGreeting()** function.

The next program, Java Example 27, demonstrates how to print "Hello World!" using a function named **greeting()** that has no input parameters and an output value of type **String** . The output value of the function is given using the **return** keyword. When the program reaches a **return** statement it exits the body of the function, and returns the function's output value to the instruction that has called that function. At that place, inside the    text = greeting();    line, the **greeting()** function to the right of the equal sign is in effect replaced by "Hello World!", the returned output value.

```
// Java Example 27
public class Main
{
        public static void main(String[] args)
        {
                String text;
                text = greeting();
                System.out.println(text);
        }

        static String greeting()
        {
                return "Hello World!";
        }
}
```

The next program, Java Example 28, demonstrates the use of a function named **lazyStudent()** (that does nothing) with an input parameter of type **String** and an output value also of type **String** .

```
// Java Example 28
public class Main
{
        public static void main(String[] args) {
                String x = "Hello World!";
                String y = lazyStudent( x );
                System.out.println( y ); }

        static String lazyStudent(String z) {
                return z; }
}
```

The next program, Java Example 29, demonstrates how to print "Hello World!" using a function named **printGreeting()** that has two input parameters of type **String** and no output value.

A shorter version of the program could use the   System.out.println( text1 + " " + text2 + "!" );   line.

```java
// Java Example 29
public class Main
{
        public static void main(String[] args)
        {
                String word1 = "Hello";
                String word2 = "World";
                printGreeting(word1, word2);
        }

        static void printGreeting(String text1, String text2)
        {
                String text = text1 + " " + text2 + "!";
                System.out.println(text);
        }
}
```

The next program, Java Example 30, demonstrates how to print "Hello World!" using a function named **greeting()** that has two input parameters of type **String** and an output value of type **String**.

A shorter version of the program could use the two lines   System.out.println( greeting(word1, word2) );   and   return text1 + " " + text2 + "!";   . An even shorter version of the program could use the System.out.println( greeting("Hello", "World") );   line.

```java
// Java Example 30
public class Main
{
        public static void main(String[] args)
        {
                String word1 = "Hello";
                String word2 = "World";
                String sentence = greeting(word1, word2);
                System.out.println(sentence);
        }

        static String greeting(String text1, String text2)
        {
                String text = text1 + " " + text2 + "!";
                return text;
        }
}
```

# 9. Java objects: methods of the Math, String, and StringBuffer classes

You have already used a method (a function) of the **Math** class, the **random()** method that returns a random number. This is a **static** method, and does not require the creation of an object. The name of the **Math** class is listed in front of the name of the **random() static** method, the two being connected by a dot. To call this method we write **Math.random()** .

You have also used a method of the **String** class, the **charAt()** method that returns the character found at a given location in a text string. This method can be called only after a **String** object has been created (instantiated). The name of the **String** object (for example, **text**) is listed in front of the name of the **charAt()** method, the two being connected by a dot. To call this method, and to find the first character in the text string named **text**, we write **text.charAt(0)** .

## 9.1. Important methods and constants of the Math class : abs() , pow() , sin() , cos() , round() , floor() , random() , PI , E

The **abs(x)** function returns the absolute value of a number, $|x|$ . The input value can be of type **byte** , **short** , **int** , **long** , **float** , or **double** . The output value can be of type **int** , **long** , **float** , or **double** , of the same type as the input value.

The **pow(x, y)** function returns a power, $x^y$ . The first input parameter **x** is the base, and the second input parameter **y** is the exponent. The base and the exponent can be of type **byte** , **short** , **int** , **long** , **float** , or **double** . The output value is a floating point number of type **double** .

The **sin(x)** function returns the sine of angle **x**, which is given in radians. The input value **x** is of type **double** , and the output value is also of type **double** .

The **cos(x)** function returns the cosine of angle **x**, which is given in radians. The input value **x** is of type **double** , and the output value is also of type **double** .

The **round(x)** function rounds up or down a number **x** to its nearest integer value. When the input value **x** is of type **float** , the output value is of type **int** . When the input value **x** is of type **double** , the output value is of type **long** .

The **floor(x)** function returns the largest integer that is less than or equal to the input parameter **x** . The input value **x** is of type **float** or **double** , and the output value is of type **double** .

Remember, when plotted on a number line, a smaller number is on the left side of a larger number.

The **random()** function, with no input parameter, returns a pseudorandom number in the [0, 1) range. The output value is of type **double** .

**Math.PI** is number $\pi$ , a constant of type **double** .

**Math.E** is Euler's number, the base of the natural logarithm, a constant of type **double** .

There are other useful **Math** methods, not required for the IB Computer Science exam: **acos()** , **asin()** , **atan()** , **cbrt()** , **ceil()** , **cosh()** , **exp()** , **log()** , **max()** , **min()** , **signum()** , **sinh()** , **sqrt()** , **tan()** , **tanh()** , **toDegrees()** , **toRadians()** . For a list of all the methods of the **Math** class, please go to: **www.tutorialspoint.com/java/lang/java_lang_math.htm**

The next program, Java Example 31, demonstrates the use of some **Math** class methods.

```
// Java Example 31
public class Main
{
        public static void main(String[] args)
        {
                System.out.println("pi = " + Math.PI);   // output : 3.141592653589793
                System.out.println("e = " + Math.E);   // output : 2.718281828459045
                System.out.println("the absolute value of -5 = " + Math.abs(-5));   // output : 5
                System.out.println("5 to the 3rd power = " + Math.pow(5, 3));   // output : 125.0
                double a = Math.PI/6;   // an angle of 30 degrees, given in radians
                System.out.println("sin( 30 deg ) = " + Math.sin(a));   // output : 0.49999999999999994
                System.out.println("cos( 30 deg ) = " + Math.cos(a));   // output : 0.8660254037844387
                System.out.println("round( 7.2 ) = " + Math.round(7.2));   // output : 7
                System.out.println("round( 7.7 ) = " + Math.round(7.7));   // output : 8
                System.out.println("floor( 8.8 ) = " + Math.floor(8.8));   // output : 8.0
                System.out.println("floor( -8.8 ) = " + Math.floor(-8.8));   // output : -9.0
                System.out.println("random number = " + Math.random());
        }
}
```

### 9.2. Important methods of the String class : equals() , substring() , length() , charAt() , indexOf() , compareTo() , toUpperCase() , toLowerCase() , format()

It is very important to realize that, even though the text string associated with a given **String** class object is not listed as an input parameter, it is indeed provided to each of these **String** class methods. These methods (with the exception of **format()** ) require an instantiated **String** object. The name of the instantiated **String** object goes in front of the name of the **String** class method, the two being separated by a dot.

The **equals(String text)** method compares the text string of the instantiated **String** object with the text string of the **text** object, and returns **true** when the two text strings are identical, or **false** otherwise. The output value is of type **boolean**.

> **Warning!** When two **String** objects are compared using the == symbol, it is not the text strings that are compared, but the addresses in RAM (the references, the pointers) of the two objects. This is also true for other Java objects, not just objects of the **String** class.

The **substring(int startPos, int endPos)** and **substring(int startPos)** methods return a part of the original text string (of the instantiated **String** object). The **startPos** index gives the position of the first alphanumeric character of the selected substring, and the **endPos** index gives the position of the first character after the selected substring. The index of the first character is 0. The output value is of type **String**. When the second argument **endPos** is missing, the selected substring goes all the way to the end of the original text string.

The **length()** method returns the number of alphanumeric characters in the text string (of the instantiated **String** object). The output value is of type **int**.

The **charAt(i)** method returns the character at the position given by index **i** in the text string (of the instantiated **String** object). The index of the first character is 0. The output value is of type **char**.

The **indexOf(String text)** method returns the first position where a given character or the text substring **text** is found inside the text string of the instantiated **String** object. If no match is found, the method returns −1. The output value is of type **int**.

The **compareTo(String text)** method compares two text strings letter by letter, starting with the first letter. If the two text strings are identical, the method returns 0. Otherwise, the method returns the difference of the Unicode values for the first time when the compared alphanumeric characters don't match. The Unicode value from **text** is subtracted from the Unicode value from the instantiated **String** object. The output value is of type **int**.

The **toUpperCase()** method changes all the letters in the instantiated **String** object to upper case. The output value is of type **String**.

The **toLowerCase()** method changes all the letters in the instantiated **String** object to lower case. The output value is of type **String**.

The **format( … )** method is a **static String** class method that returns a formatted text string. Because it is **static** , it does not require an instantiated **String** object, like the other **String** class methods presented here. The output value is of type **String**. This method is not required for the IB CS exam.

The general pattern of a format specifier is **%[flags][width][.precision]conversion_character** , where the parameters in square brackets are optional.

The flags used by **format()** are:

- = left-justify ( default is to right-justify )

+ = write a "+" sign in front of positive numerical values

0 = write "0" characters in front of numerical values, for padding

, = use coma as a grouping separator for numerical values greater than one thousand

  = write a " " (space) in front of positive numerical values

The width is the minimum number of alphanumeric characters to be written out.

The precision is the number of decimal places in a floating point number.

The conversion characters used by **format()** are:

%d = decimal number

%f = floating point number

%c = character          ( %C for upper case letter )

%s = text string          ( %S for upper case letters everywhere in the text string )

%h = hashcode          ( A hashcode is a Java substitute for the hidden RAM address. )

%n = newline          ( \n can be used as well, with less compatibility )

There are other useful **String** methods, not required for the IB Computer Science  exam: **concat()** , **equalsIgnoreCase()** , **isEmpty()** , **lastIndexOf()** , **replace()** , **replaceAll()** , **toCharArray()** , **valueOf()** . For a list of all the methods of the **String** class, please go to:
**www.tutorialspoint.com/java/java_strings.htm**

The next program, Java Example 32, demonstrates the use of some **String** class methods.

```java
// Java Example 32
public class Main
{
        public static void main(String[] args)
        {
                String object1 = "pineapple";
                String object2 = "apple";
                System.out.print("comparing " + object1 + " to " + object2 + " : ");
                System.out.println( object1.equals(object2) );
                String object3 = object1.substring(2,4);
                System.out.println("substring extracted : " + object3);
                String object4 = object1.substring(4);
                System.out.println("substring extracted : " + object4);
                System.out.print("comparing " + object2 + " to " + object4 + " : ");
                System.out.println( object2.equals(object4) );
                System.out.print("comparing the object references : ");
                System.out.println( object2 == object4 );
                System.out.println("length of " + object1 + " : " + object1.length() );
                System.out.println("first letter of " + object2 + " : " + object2.charAt(0) );
                System.out.println("position of pl in " + object2 + " : " + object2.indexOf("pl") );
                System.out.println("position of z in " + object1 + " : " + object1.indexOf('z') );
                System.out.print("comparing " + object1 + " to " + object2 + " : ");
                System.out.println( object1.compareTo(object2) );
                System.out.println("subtracting Unicode values : " + ( (int) 'p' - (int) 'a' ) );
                String object5 = object1.toUpperCase();
                System.out.println("converting " + object1 + " to upper case : " + object5);
                String object6 = object5.toLowerCase();
                System.out.println("converting " + object5 + " to lower case : " + object6);
                String object7 = String.format(" %d and %f make %s ", 10, 20.0, "30");
                System.out.println(object7);
                String object8 = String.format("%+10.5f", 3.1415926535);
                System.out.println("pi is " + object8 + " in this approximation");
        }
}
```

The program also demonstrates the use of the type casting operator **(int)** . By writing **(int)** in front of the characters **'p'** and **'a'** we force the computer to convert these characters into their Unicode integer values. The difference of these integer values has to be inside parentheses, because we want the computer to perform the subtraction first, before the text string concatenation operator "+" changes the **(int) 'p'** integer number into a **String** object. What is the value of **(int) 'p'** after the conversion into a text string? Can the subtraction operator "-" be used in between two **String** objects?

## 9.3. Important methods of the StringBuffer class : equals() , substring() , length() , charAt() , indexOf() , compareTo()

The **StringBuffer** class is more powerful than the **String** class. It is designed for text strings that change often. Objects of the **String** class are said to be immutable, this means that  when an old **String** object is modified the Java program has to place the new **String** object into a new location in RAM, while the old **String** object, unmodified, keeps its old place in RAM. When **StringBuffer** objects are modified they stay in the same place in RAM. This increases the speed of the Java program, and also reduces the amount of computer memory that is used.

**Warning!** Unlike an object of the **String** class, for which there is a shortcut, an object of the **StringBuffer** class has to be created using the **new** keyword and the **StringBuffer()** constructor.

Notice the different ways in which a **String** object and a **StringBuffer** object are instantiated:

String fruit = "banana";   with shortcut and   StringBuffer fruit = new StringBuffer("banana");   without.

It is very important to realize that, even though the text string associated with a given **StringBuffer** class object is not listed as an input parameter, it is indeed provided to each of these **StringBuffer** class methods. These methods require an instantiated **StringBuffer** object. The name of the instantiated **StringBuffer** object goes in front of the name of the **StringBuffer** class method, the two being separated by a dot.

The **equals(StringBuffer text)** method compares the text string of the instantiated **StringBuffer** object with the text string of the **text** object, and returns **true** when the two text strings are identical, or **false** otherwise. The output value is of type **boolean**.

**Warning!** Do not use the == symbol to compare the text strings stored in two **StringBuffer** objects!

The **substring(int startPos, int endPos)** and **substring(int startPos)** methods return a part of the original text string (of the instantiated **StringBuffer** object). The **startPos** index gives the position of the first alphanumeric character of the selected substring, and the **endPos** index gives the position of the first character after the selected substring. The index of the first character is 0. The output value is of type **String**. Remember, the output value is not of type **StringBuffer** . When the second argument **endPos** is missing, the selected substring goes all the way to the end of the original text string.

The **length()** method returns the number of alphanumeric characters in the text string (of the instantiated **StringBuffer** object). The output value is of type **int**.

The **charAt(i)** method returns the character at the position given by index **i** in the text string (of the instantiated **StringBuffer** object). The index of the first character is 0. The output value is of type **char**.

The **indexOf(String text)** method returns the first position where a given character or the text substring **text** is found inside the text string of the instantiated **StringBuffer** object. If no match is found, the method returns –1. The output value is of type **int**.

The **compareTo(StringBuffer text)** method compares two text strings letter by letter, starting with the first letter. If the two text strings are identical, the method returns 0. Otherwise, the method returns the difference of the Unicode values for the first time when the compared alphanumeric characters don't match. The Unicode value from **text** is subtracted from the Unicode value from the instantiated **StringBuffer** object. The output value is of type **int**.

There are other useful **StringBuffer** methods, not required for the IB Computer Science  exam: **append()** , **reverse()** , **delete()** , **insert()** , **replace()** . For a list of all the methods of the **StringBuffer** class, please go to: **www.tutorialspoint.com/java/java_string_buffer.htm**

## 10. Java objects: introduction to Object-Oriented Programming

### 10.1. The constructor

A very important method (function) of a Java class is its constructor. The constructor is called every time an object of a given class is created (instantiated), and space in RAM is reserved for that object using the **new** keyword. The constructor has the same name as its class. The constructor is the only method that does not have an output value type (a return type), not even **void** . A class may have one or more constructors. Very often the constructor is used to give initial values to the field variables of the newly created object. If no constructor is implemented in the program, then Java will use a default constructor, one that initializes the field variables to their default values (zero, null, etc.).

The next program, Java Example 33, prints the "Hello World!" message using the constructor of a Java object.

```
// Java Example 33
public class Main
{
        public static void main(String[] args)
        {
                MyHello greeting;
                greeting = new MyHello();
        }
}

class MyHello
{
        public MyHello()   // the constructor
        {
                System.out.println("Hello World!");
        }
}
```

We notice that in addition to the **Main** class we also have another class named **MyHello**. The **MyHello** class is not **public**, since one Java source file can contain only one **public** class. Remember, the name of the **public** class must match the name of the Java source file. We could make the **MyHello** class **public** by writing its Java code in a separate Java source file, if we wanted that. Then the two Java source files would be part of the same package.

The **MyHello** class has only one function (method), just like the **Main** class, but there is one big difference: the **MyHello()** function is not **static**, like the **main()** function. This means that we cannot call the **MyHello()** function until we create (instantiate) an object of type **MyHello** . The **greeting** object, of type **MyHello** , is declared and created (instantiated) in the **main()** function. The **new** keyword reserves memory in RAM for the newly created object. The address where this object is located in RAM is held in **greeting** , which now also serves as an object reference (memory address, pointer). In other words, **greeting** is the name of a Java object and at the same time it is the name of a pointer variable that holds the memory address of that object. The **greeting** object is initialized with the help of its constructor. The **MyHello()** constructor has the same name as the **MyHello** class, and has no return type of any kind, not even **void** .

The declaration, instantiation, and initialization of the **greeting** object could also be done in just one line:  MyHello greeting = new MyHello();  Another option that produces the same "Hello World!" message on the computer screen is to type just  new MyHello();  , but since in this later case we do not save the memory address where we can find the newly created object, this object will soon disappear from RAM when Java does the garbage collection.

### 10.2. Accessing members of a class or object from a different class or object

The next program, Java Example 34, prints the "Hello World!" message using a user defined method of a Java object. The Java **greeting** object of the **MyHello** class has a default constructor, another function named **printGreeting()** , and a text string object (a field variable) named **myText** . The Java program demonstrates how the variables, functions, and objects of a given instantiated object can be accessed from another instantiated object or **static** method. We do this by writing the name of the instantiated object and a dot in front of the name of the desired variable, function, or object. For example, inside the body of the **main()** method, we use the **greeting.myText** and **greeting.printGreeting()** expressions.

```java
// Java Example 34
public class Main
{
        public static void main(String[] args)
        {
                MyHello greeting;
                greeting = new MyHello();
                greeting.myText = "Hello World!";
                greeting.printGreeting();
        }
}

class MyHello
{
        String myText;

        public void printGreeting()
        {
                System.out.println(myText);
        }
}
```

Can we print the same "Hello World!" message without ever instantiating an object of type **MyHello** ? Yes, but in this case the **myText** object and the **printGreeting()** function of the **MyHello** class need to be declared **static** . The **static** members of a class exist in only one copy, even if no object of that class is instantiated.

The next program, Java Example 35, demonstrates how the **static** variables, functions, and objects of a given class can be accessed from another instantiated object or **static** method. We do this by writing the name of the class and a dot in front of the name of the desired **static** variable, function, or object. For example, inside the body of the **main()** method, we use the **MyHello.myText** and **MyHello.printGreeting()** expressions.

```
// Java Example 35
public class Main
{
        public static void main(String[] args)
        {
                MyHello.myText = "Hello World!";
                MyHello.printGreeting();
        }
}

class MyHello
{
        static String myText;

        public static void printGreeting()
        {
                System.out.println(myText);
        }
}
```

**10.3. Encapsulation**

In many situations we do not want the **static** methods of other classes, or the methods of other instantiated objects, to have direct access to the variables, methods, or objects of a given instantiated object. In such a situation we use the **private** keyword in front of those protected variables, methods, or objects. This is an important Object-Oriented Programming (OOP) feature called encapsulation .

The next program, Java Example 36, demonstrates how to use the input parameters of the constructor in order to initialize the protected ( **private** ) field variables of a newly created object. In this example there is only one such **private** field variable, the **String** object named **myText** .

```java
// Java Example 36
public class Main
{
        public static void main(String[] args)
        {
                MyHello greeting;
                greeting = new MyHello("Hello World!");
                greeting.printGreeting();
        }
}


class MyHello
{
        private String myText;

        public MyHello(String text)   // the constructor
        {
                myText = text;
        }

        public void printGreeting()
        {
                System.out.println(myText);
        }
}
```

Inside the **MyHello** class we could also refer to the **String** object **myText** as **this.myText** . Inside the Java program we could write   this.myText = text;   instead of   myText = text;   , and we could write System.out.println(this.myText);   instead of   System.out.println(myText);   , and it would make no difference. The **this** keyword stands for the name of the actual object (for instantiated objects), and it is very useful when we have two variables or objects with the same name, and we need to distinguish between them. The actual instantiated object, in this Java program, is **greeting** . In general, one could create (instantiate) more than just one object of the **MyHello** class, and then the **this** keyword will refer to whatever actual object is being accessed by the Java program.

In the next program, Java Example 37, inside the body of the **myHello()** constructor, the **myText** name refers to the formal parameter **myText** (which used to be named **text** in the Java Example 36 program), and not to the **private String** object **myText** (which now has to be accessed using the **this** keyword).

```
// Java Example 37
public class Main
{
        public static void main(String[] args)
        {
                MyHello greeting = new MyHello("Hello World!");
                greeting.printGreeting();
        }
}


class MyHello
{
        private String myText;   // the field variable myText is defined

        public MyHello(String myText)   // the formal parameter myText is defined
        {
                this.myText = myText;
        }

        public void printGreeting()
        {
                System.out.println(myText);
        }
}
```

The Java program would not work as intended if, instead of writing   this.myText = myText;   , we wrote   myText = myText;   . This should be obvious, based on logic. Just think about it. How could the Java compiler figure out that the first time **myText** stands for the **private** field variable, while the second time **myText** stands for the formal parameter? No way!

Since a formal parameter exists only inside the body of the function where it is defined, we do not have the same situation inside the **printGreeting()** function, where **myText** unambiguously refers to the **private String** object **myText.** Here, inside the **printGreeting()** function, we could write System.out.println(this.myText);   instead of   System.out.println(myText);   , and it would make no difference.


## 10.4. Method overloading


**Method overloading** is an Object-Oriented Programing (OOP) feature that allows a class to have two or more methods with the same name, as long as the methods have different input parameters. The methods can be distinguished when they have a different number of input parameters, or when they have input parameters of different types. It is not allowed to have two methods with the same input parameters, but with different output value types (return types). Method overloading is an example of **compile time polymorphism**, because Java decides which one of the methods to use at compile time, based on the number and types of the input parameters. A very common example of method overloading is when a class has two or more different constructors.

The next program, Java Example 38, demonstrates a Java class with two constructors. The first constructor, with no input parameters, is called a **no-argument constructor** . The second constructor, with an input parameter of type **String** , is called a **parameterized constructor** .

```java
// Java Example 38
public class Main
{
        public static void main(String[] args)
        {
                MyHello greeting1, greeting2;
                greeting1 = new MyHello();
                greeting1.printGreeting();
                greeting2 = new MyHello("Hello World!");
                greeting2.printGreeting();
        }
}

class MyHello
{
        private String myText;

        public MyHello()   // the first (no-argument) constructor
        {
                myText = "Have a good day!";
        }

        public MyHello(String text)   // the second (parameterized) constructor
        {
                myText = text;
        }

        public void printGreeting()
        {
                System.out.println(myText);
        }
}
```

The Java program will print "Have a good day!" first, because the first object is created (instantiated) using the first (no-argument) constructor, and then it will print "Hello World!", because the second object is created (instantiated) using the second (parameterized) constructor.

The next program, Java Example 39, also demonstrates a Java class with two constructors. In this example the **ConstructorExample** class has two field variables, one **String** object named **name** and one **int** variable named **age**, that are not **private**. As a consequence, these two field variables can be accessed directly from the **main()** method of the **Main** class.

```java
// Java Example 39
public class Main
{
        public static void main(String[] args)
        {
                ConstructorExample o1 = new ConstructorExample();
                ConstructorExample o2 = new ConstructorExample("Ken", 21);
                System.out.println("My name is " + o1.name + " and my age is " + o1.age + ".");
                System.out.println("My name is " + o2.name + " and my age is " + o2.age + ".");
        }
}

class ConstructorExample
{
        String name;
        int age;

        ConstructorExample()
        {
                name = "Barbie";
                age = 18;
        }

        ConstructorExample(String n, int a)
        {
                name = n;
                age = a;
        }
}
```

The Java program will print "My name is Barbie and my age is 18." first, because the first object **o1** is created (instantiated) using the first (no-argument) constructor, and then it will print "My name is Ken and my age is 21.", because the second object **o2** is created (instantiated) using the second (parameterized) constructor.

*"On the Internet, nobody knows you're a dog."*

**Warning!** Never take for granted the age that is self-reported by a Ken or a Barbie! Especially if this information comes from a computer (or cellphone) screen, without previous direct visual contact between the involved parties. Never take for granted even the name that is self-reported by a person that you have never met face-to-face before.

# 11. Variables: instance variables and static variables

We have used a **static String** object earlier, in Java Example 35. Static field variables exist in only one copy. Now, in order to better understand the behavior of **static** variables inside their objects, we show a program, Java Example 40, in which three objects are instantiated. These three objects ( **obj1** , **obj2** , and **obj3** ) share the same **static int** variable named **myStaticVar**. Changing this variable in any one of the three objects will change it in all three objects. The name of an instantiated object is not even needed, we can access the static variable using the name of the class instead, which in this case is **StaticVarExample**. To **access** a variable means to be able to find (read) and change (write) its value.

```java
// Java Example 40
public class Main
{
        public static void main(String[] args)
        {
                StaticVarExample obj1 = new StaticVarExample();
                StaticVarExample obj2 = new StaticVarExample();
                StaticVarExample obj3 = new StaticVarExample();

                System.out.println(obj1.myStaticVar);   // output : 123
                System.out.println(obj2.myStaticVar);   // output : 123
                System.out.println(obj3.myStaticVar);   // output : 123
                System.out.println("");   // new line

                // change the value of the static variable in object obj2
                obj2.myStaticVar = 505;

                System.out.println(obj1.myStaticVar);   // output : 505
                System.out.println(obj2.myStaticVar);   // output : 505
                System.out.println(obj3.myStaticVar);   // output : 505
                System.out.println("");   // new line

                // the name of an instantiated object is not even needed
                StaticVarExample.myStaticVar = 456;
                System.out.println(StaticVarExample.myStaticVar);   // output : 456
        }
}

class StaticVarExample
{
        public static int myStaticVar = 123;
}
```

Field variables that are not **static** are called instance variables. When a field variable is not **static** , each created (instantiated) object will have its own copy of that instance variable. The instance variables are independent of each other, and they can be accessed only by using the name of the instantiated object they belong to, followed by a dot. Trying to access an instance variable by using the name of the class will produce a compiler error.

The next program, Java Example 41, is similar to Java Example 40, with one important difference: the **int** variable named **myInstanceVar** of the **InstanceVarExample** class is not **static** . As a result, changing the value of this integer variable in the **obj2** object will not modify its value in the **obj1** and **obj3** objects.

```java
// Java Example 41
public class Main
{
        public static void main(String[] args)
        {
                InstanceVarExample obj1 = new InstanceVarExample();
                InstanceVarExample obj2 = new InstanceVarExample();
                InstanceVarExample obj3 = new InstanceVarExample();

                System.out.println(obj1.myInstanceVar);   // output : 123
                System.out.println(obj2.myInstanceVar);   // output : 123
                System.out.println(obj3.myInstanceVar);   // output : 123
                System.out.println("");   // new line

                // change the value of the static variable in object obj2
                obj2.myInstanceVar = 505;

                System.out.println(obj1.myInstanceVar);   // output : 123
                System.out.println(obj2.myInstanceVar);   // output : 505
                System.out.println(obj3.myInstanceVar);   // output : 123
        }
}

class InstanceVarExample
{
        public int myInstanceVar = 123;
}
```

## 12. Java objects: 1D and 2D arrays

In Java one dimensional (1D) arrays are objects that hold a given number of elements of the same type, stored in memory in a sequential order. These elements can be variables of a primitive type, or objects of a given class. First an array has to be declared. In this way the Java compiler gets to know the name of the array and the data type of the array elements. Then the array has to be instantiated. At this step the Java compiler reserves space in RAM for the array, and gives the array elements their default values (zero, null, etc.). After these two steps the array elements can be reassigned new values. The elements of the array are identified with the help of an index, an integer counter that starts from zero, like this:
**array_name[index]**

> **Warning!** The fact that in Java the array index starts at zero can be a little confusing, especially since in mathematics and in some other programming languages (for example in Pascal) the array index starts at one. For the same reason the index of the last element in a Java array with n elements is not n, but n–1.

fb.com/programmingjokes                    **NERD** *4* **LIFE**.studio

The **declaration** of an array can be done in two equivalent ways:

**data_type[] array_name;**

**data_type array_name[];**

the first method being the preferred one.

The **instantiation** of an array is done in this way:

**array_name = new data_type[size];**

where the size of the array is the number of elements stored in the array.

The declaration and instantiation statements can be combined into just one:

**data_type[] array_name = new data_type[size];**

Java arrays have one very important field variable (property) called **length** . This is an integer variable that holds the size of the array, which is the number of elements stored in the array.

The next program, Java Example 42, demonstrates the use of an array of integer elements.

```
// Java Example 42
public class Main
{
        public static void main (String[] args)
        {
                int[] pi_digits;   // declaration
                pi_digits = new int[5];   // instantiation
                pi_digits[0] = 3;   // initialization
                pi_digits[1] = 1;
                pi_digits[2] = 4;
                pi_digits[3] = 1;
                pi_digits[4] = 6;
                System.out.println ("The array has " + pi_digits.length + " elements.");
                System.out.print("pi = " + pi_digits[0] + ".");
                for(int i=1; i<=4; i=i+1) System.out.print( pi_digits[i] );
        }
}
```

If, at the moment when an array is created, all the arrays elements are given some known initial values, then there is an alternative shorter way to define, instantiate, and initialize the array.

**data_type[] array_name = { element0, element1, element2, ... };**

In this situation there is no need to use the **new** keyword, or to specify the number of array elements.

The next program, Java Example 43, demonstrates the shorter way of creating an array of integer numbers, when all the array elements have known initial values.

```
// Java Example 43
public class Main
{
        public static void main (String[] args)
        {
                int[] pi_digits = { 3, 1, 4, 1, 5, 9, 2, 6, 5, 3, 5 };
                System.out.println ("The array has " + pi_digits.length + " elements.");
                System.out.print("pi = " + pi_digits[0] + ".");
                for(int i=1; i<=10; i=i+1) System.out.print( pi_digits[i] );
        }
}
```

The next program, Java Example 44, demonstrates the use of an array of **String** elements.

```
// Java Example 44
public class Main
{
        public static void main (String[] args)
        {
                String[] week = new String[7];
                week[0] = "Monday";
                week[1] = "Tuesday";
                week[2] = "Wednesday";
                week[3] = "Thursday";
                week[4] = "Friday";
                week[5] = "Saturday";
                week[6] = "Sunday";
                System.out.println ("The week has " + week.length + " days.");
                for(int i=0; i<=6; i=i+1) System.out.println( week[i] );
        }
}
```

When all the elements on an array are accessed in sequential order, from the first one to the last one, there is a shorter way of running the **for** loop, which is called the **for-each** loop:

**for( data_type element_name : array_name ) { ... instructions ... }**

The next program, Java Example 45, demonstrates the shorter way of creating an array of **String** elements with known initial values, and the shorter way of running the **for-each** loop that prints out, in sequential order, all the text strings stored in this **String[]** array.

```
// Java Example 45
public class Main
{
        public static void main (String[] args)
        {
                String[] week = { "Monday", "Tuesday", "Wednesday", "Thursday",
                        "Friday", "Saturday", "Sunday" };
                System.out.println ("The week has " + week.length + " days.");
                for( String day : week ) System.out.println( day );
        }
}
```

The **Java.util.Arrays** class has some useful **static** methods that work with arrays. The **binarySearch()** method searches for an element in a sorted array, using the binary search algorithm. The **equals()** method compares two arrays, to determine if they have the same elements. The **fill()** method assigns the same specified value to each array element. The **sort()** method places all the array elements in ascending order. For a list of all the methods of the **Java.util.Arrays** class, please go to **https://www.tutorialspoint.com/java/util/java_util_arrays.htm** .

> **Warning!** A **run time error** will stop the Java program whenever we have an array element with an index out of bounds. In technical language we say that **an exception is thrown**. There are special ways to **catch the exception**, handle it, and thus prevent the Java program from stopping, but such advanced programming techniques are not described here because they are not needed for the IB CS exam. You can still learn this from other sources. There is no out of bounds error for your love of computer science.

The next program, Java Example 46, demonstrates the run time error caused by an array element with an index out of bounds.

```java
// Java Example 46
public class Main
{
        public static void main (String[] args)
        {
                int[] digits = { 0, 1, 2, 3, 4, 5, 6, 7, 8, 9 };
                System.out.println( digits[0] );   // output : 0
                System.out.println( digits[9] );   // output : 9
                System.out.println( digits[13] );   // error
        }
}
```

But why won't the Java compiler catch the index out of bounds error in Java Example 46, why don't we get a **compile time error** instead? Because in Java arrays are **dynamically allocated**, meaning that their size, and the space that they will take in RAM, are not always known at compile time. For this reason it was decided that the Java interpreter will have to look for array elements with indices out of bounds.

The next program, Java Example 47, demonstrates the run time error caused by an array element with an index out of bounds. This time the size of the array is not known at compile time. Depending on the size decided at run time, the error may happen or not.

```java
// Java Example 47
import java.util.Scanner;
public class Main
{
        public static void main (String[] args)
        {
                Scanner kbdInput = new Scanner(System.in);
                System.out.print("size of array = ? ");   // input : type 10 or 20
                int size = kbdInput.nextInt();
                int[] digits = new int[size];
                for(int i=0; i<size; i=i+1)   digits[i] = i;
                System.out.println( digits[0] );   // output : 0
                System.out.println( digits[9] );   // output : 9
                System.out.println( digits[13] );   // error when the size is 10
        }
}
```

Not all programming languages check for array elements with an index out of bounds. For example, C and C++ programs will not report an error, but instead will read from or write into the wrong memory location. From this point of view Java provides a much safer option.

We can also have two dimensional (2D) arrays, also known as matrices. Elements in matrices are ordered in rows and columns. Elements in 2D arrays are identified with the help of two indices, two integer counters that start from zero. We usually think of the first index as the row index, and the second index as the column index. We can also have three dimensional (3D) arrays, or with more dimensions. The number of dimensions in an array is given by the number of closed square brackets [].

The declaration of a 2D array can be done in three equivalent ways:

**data_type[][] array_name;**

**data_type array_name[][];**

**data_type[] array_name[];**

The last method of declaring an array is in fact revealing that in Java a 2D array is an 1D array of 1D arrays. For a 2D array with elements **array_name[row][column]** , **array_name.length** gives the number of rows, and **array_name[row].length** gives the number of elements (the number of columns) in the row named **row**.

---

**Warning!** In Java there are different measurements of length that could easily get mixed up. The field variable **array_name.length** gives the length (the number of elements) of an array. The method **string_name.length()** gives the length (the number of alphanumeric characters) of a text string (an object of type **String**).

---

The next program, Java Example 48, demonstrates the use of a 2D array of integer numbers. The program shows that, when an array of integer numbers is created, all the elements have the initial value of zero. The program also shows how the number of rows and the number of columns of a 2D array can be obtained with the help of the **length** property.

```
// Java Example 48
public class Main
{
        public static void main(String[] args)
        {
                int[][] board = new int[10][20];
                board[5][15] = 505;
                System.out.println( board[5][15] );   // output : 505
                System.out.println( board[6][16] );   // output : 0 , the initial value
                System.out.println( board.length );   // output : 10 , the number of rows
                System.out.println( board[0].length );   // output : 20 , the number of columns
        }
}
```

A surprising feature of Java is that we can have a 2D array with rows of different length. While a 2D array has a well-defined number of rows, sometimes it does not have an equally well defined number of columns. In that case we can only talk about the number of elements in each individual row.

The next program, Java Example 49, demonstrates the use of a 2D array of integer numbers that are placed in rows of different length. The array **fifi** has five rows, but no defined number of columns. The Java Example 49 program also demonstrates how to create such an array in just one step, when all the elements have known initial values.

```java
// Java Example 49
public class Main
{
        public static void main(String[] args)
        {
                int[][] fifi = {{1}, {2, 3}, {4, 5, 6}, {7, 8}, {9}};
                System.out.println("The number of rows :  " + fifi.length);
                for(int i=0; i<fifi.length; i=i+1)
                {
                        System.out.print("The number of elements in row " + i);
                        System.out.println(" :  " + fifi[i].length);
                        System.out.print("The element(s) in row " + i + " :  ");
                        for(int j=0; j<fifi[i].length; j=j+1)  System.out.print(fifi[i][j] + " ");
                        System.out.println("");
                }
        }
}
```

## 13. Functions: call by value and call by reference

When a function is called, there are two ways in which the input parameters can be provided. The first option is to give the function a copy of the values of the input parameters. This is a call by value. The second option is to give the function the addresses (the references) where the input parameters are stored in RAM. This is a call by reference.

> In Java, primitive variables and objects of class **String** are always given to a function using a call by value.

The next program, Java Example 50 , demonstrates how a call by value works. The integer variable **x** inside the **main()** function is not changed by the   x = x + 100;   line inside the **addOneHundred()** function. In truth, here we deal with two independent variables, both named **x**, but existing inside the bodies of different functions. The **x** variable inside the **main()** function is what we call the actual parameter, and the **x** variable inside the **addOneHundred()** function is what we call the formal parameter. The place in a computer program where a variable lives (where the variable exists, where it can be accessed) is called the variable scope.

```java
// Java Example 50
public class Main
{
        public static void main(String[] args)
        {
                int x = 505;
                System.out.println("before the function call : x = " + x);   // output : 505
                int y = addOneHundred(x);
                System.out.println("after the function call : x = " + x);   // output : 505
        }

        static int addOneHundred(int x)
        {
                x = x + 100;
                return x;
        }
}
```

One could rename the formal parameter, making it very clear that the program works with two different variables. For example, the **addOneHundred()** function could be changed into:

```java
static int addOneHundred(int z)
{
        z = z + 100;
        return z;
}
```

When this **addOneHundred()** function is called by value, the value of the actual parameter **x** is copied into the formal parameter **z**. In this way the value of **x** is not changed.

The next program, Java Example 51 , demonstrates how a call by value works. The **String** object named **greeting** inside the **main()** function is not changed by the   greeting = "Hello Universe!";   line in the **printGreeting()** function.

```java
// Java Example 51
public class Main
{
        public static void main(String[] args)
        {
                String greeting = "Hello World!";
                printGreeting(greeting);   // output : Hello World!
                printGreeting(greeting);   // output : Hello World!
        }

        static void printGreeting(String greeting)
        {
                System.out.println(greeting);
                greeting = "Hello Universe!";
        }
}
```

In Java, objects (that are not of class **String**) and arrays are always given to a function using a call by reference.

The next program, Java Example 52 , demonstrates how a call by reference works. The array of integer numbers named **myArray** is given to the **addOneHundred()** function using a call by reference. As a result the value of the integer variable stored in **myArray[2]** changes. As a matter of fact, the values of all the elements stored in **myArray** go up by one hundred.

```java
// Java Example 52
public class Main
{
        public static void main(String[] args)
        {
                int[] myArray = { 10, 20, 30, 40, 50 };
                System.out.println("before the function call : " + myArray[2]);   // output : 30
                addOneHundred(myArray);
                System.out.println("after the function call : " + myArray[2]);   // output : 130
        }

        public static void addOneHundred(int[] z)
        {
                int n = z.length;
                for(int i = 0; i < n; i = i + 1)   z[i] = z[i] + 100;
        }
}
```

The next program, Java Example 53 , demonstrates how a call by reference works. The object named **x** of type (of class) **MyNumber** is given to the **addOneHundred()** function using a call by reference. As a result the value of the integer variable stored in **x.number** changes.

```java
// Java Example 53
public class Main
{
        public static void main(String[] args)
        {
                MyNumber x = new MyNumber(300);
                System.out.println("before the function call : " + x.number);   // output : 300
                addOneHundred(x);
                System.out.println("after the function call : " + x.number);   // output : 400
        }

        public static void addOneHundred(MyNumber z)
        {
                z.number = z.number + 100;
        }
}

class MyNumber
{
        int number;

        public MyNumber(int y)   // the constructor
        {
                number = y;
        }
}
```

Calling a function using a **call by reference** is a powerful programming technique. It allows us to give a positive answer to questions like: "Can an input variable be also used as an output variable?" and "Can a function return more than one output parameter?". With this great power, however, comes great responsibility. It is very easy to make a mistake and, as a result, change the value of an input variable that was meant to stay the same. For this reason in Java the programmer does not have direct access to the actual address in memory of an object or array. Instead, the name of the object or array also substitutes for the name of the address in RAM (the **reference**, the pointer) of that object or array. While, for example, in C and C++ the programmer can find the address in memory of a variable, using the **&** operator, this is not possible in Java. While, for example, in C and C++ the content of a location in memory can be modified using the **\*** operator, this is not possible in Java. In Java there are no pointers. From this point of view Java is a safer language, but not as powerful as other programming languages that provide unrestricted access to anything in RAM.

# 14. Java programs with command line parameters

A program with command line parameters is executed in a Command Prompt window. Please review Chapter 1, Three options for running the HelloWorld Java program, Section 1.4, The Command Line Interface option ( javac.exe and java.exe ). That program, **HelloWorld.java** , did not use any command line parameters. Now you will type, compile, and run a new Java program, called **MyNameIs.java** , that takes the name of a person (made of one, two, or more words) as the command line input.

Step 1. Go to the **C:\ JavaPrograms** folder that you have created in Chapter 1.

Step 2. Inside the **JavaPrograms** folder create a new text file. Right-click with the mouse, then select **New|Text Document**. Change the name of the text file from **New Text Document.txt** to **MyNameIs.java** . The computer will give you a warning message that you should ignore.

> **Warning!** Sometimes you cannot see the file name extension, and as a result you cannot change it from **.txt** to **.java** . To make the file name extension visible you should search for **Folder Options** (in Windows 8) or **File Explorer Options** (in Windows 10), and then uncheck the **Hide extensions for files of known type** check box.

Step 3. Using **Notepad**, open the **MyNameIs.java** source file, type the code of the Java Example 54 program, listed on the next page, and then save the file and close Notepad.

> At this time you should recognize **String[] args** , the input parameter of the **main()** method, as an array of **String** objects. This array of text strings holds all the command line parameters. We can find the number of command line parameters in **args** by checking the **args.length** property of this array. The command line parameters, if they exist, are accessed using **args[0]** , **args[1]** , ... etc.

Step 4. Open a Command Prompt window. Search for Command Prompt if you need to find it.

Step 5a. Type **cd C:\JavaPrograms**<ENTER>. This will move the command prompt to the **JavaPrograms** directory (folder), which becomes the current directory.

Step 5b. Type **dir**<ENTER>. This will show all the files and folders in the current directory (folder). You should see the **MyNameIs.java** source file there.

Step 5c. Type **set path=C:\Program Files\Java\jdk1.8.0_111\bin**<ENTER> with no extra spaces. This will tell the computer where to find the **javac.exe** and the **java.exe** executable files.

> **Warning!** If you have a different version of the Java Development Kit (JDK) installed, then you will have to modify the numbers in the above path accordingly.

Step 5d. Type **javac MyNameIs.java**<ENTER>. The **javac.exe** compiler will compile the Java source file into Bytecode language, and then it will save the compiled output into a **.class** file.

Step 5e. Type **dir**<ENTER>. Verify that the **MyNameIs.class** file is indeed there.

Step 5f. Type **java MyNameIs**<ENTER>. The **java.exe** interpreter (the Java Virtual Machine) will turn the Bytecode into machine code, and then the machine code will get executed, one instruction at a time. The machine code is specific to the computer that runs the program, but since the Bytecode language is very close to the actual machine code language, the **java.exe** interpreter is super-fast.

Step 5g. Type **java MyNameIs** again, but this time followed by one, two, or more names (or words) before you hit <ENTER>.

```java
// Java Example 54
public class MyNameIs
{
        public static void main(String[] args)
        {
                int n = args.length;
                if (n==0)
                {
                        System.out.println("Please type: java MyNameIs firstname lastname");
                }
                else if (n==1)
                {
                        System.out.println("Nice to meet you, " + args[0] + ".");
                        System.out.println("I don't think I remember your last name.");
                }
                else if (n==2)
                {
                        System.out.println("Nice to meet you, " + args[0] + " " + args[1] + ".");
                        System.out.println("Your first name matches perfectly your last name.");
                }
                else
                {
                        System.out.print ("You have a very long name,");
                        for(int i=0; i<n; i++)   {   System.out.print(" " + args[i]);   }
                        System.out.println(".");
                        System.out.println("But this is not your fault, of course!");
                }

        }
}
```

A successful compilation and execution of the **MyNameIs** program looks like this:

## 15. Java objects: the ArrayList and the LinkedList classes

Java has two important classes that can be used to handle a list of objects. These are the **ArrayList** and the **LinkedList** classes, both implemented in the **java.util** package. Instantiated objects of the **ArrayList** and **LinkedList** classes can be used to implement a general type of list, a stack, or a queue.

### 15.1. The ArrayList class

The objects in an **ArrayList** list are ordered by index, just like the elements of an array. The advantage of this implementation is that the objects are very quickly accessed, the Java program knows where the objects are in RAM, based on their index. The disadvantage of this implementation is that when an old object is deleted from the list, or when a new object is inserted into the list, all the other subsequent objects have to change their locations in RAM, because their index changes. Unlike an array of objects, the size of an **ArrayList** list can increase in order to accommodate more objects added to the list.

The next program, Java Example 55, demonstrates how an **ArrayList** list is created, populated with objects of type **String**, **Float**, or **Integer**, and how these objects are then listed in order. Notice the two different ways in which the list elements can be printed, by using the **for** loop or by using the list name.

```
// Java Example 55
import java.util.ArrayList;
public class Main
{
        public static void main(String[] args)
        {
                ArrayList myList = new ArrayList();
                myList.add("apple");   // the object with index 0
                myList.add("banana");   // the object with index 1
                myList.add(3.1416);   // the object with index 2
                myList.add(4);   // the object with index 3
                myList.add("coconut");   // the object with index 4
                myList.add("pumpkin");   // the object with index 5
                for(int i=0; i<6; i=i+1)
                        System.out.println( myList.get(i) );
                myList.remove(4);   // remove the object with index 4, "coconut"
                myList.remove("banana");   // remove the object "banana"
                myList.remove(3.1416);   // remove the object 3.1416
                System.out.println("");
                System.out.println(myList);
                myList.add(1, "cheese");   // add the object "cheese" in the second place
                myList.add(0, "steak");   // add the object "steak" in the first place
                myList.add(5, 505);   // add the object 505 in the last place
                System.out.println("");
                System.out.println(myList);
        }
}
```

> **Warning!** Objects of type **Float** or **Integer** are not the same thing as primitive variables of type **float** or **int**. An **Integer** object contains a **long** variable and some auxiliary methods. We say that the **Integer** class is a **wrapper class**. You will find more information about the Java wrapper classes in Chapter 16.

Please notice that the    myList.remove(4);    line does not remove the **Integer** object 4, but instead it removes the **String** object "coconut", whose index is equal to 4.

If all the objects in a list are of the same class, for example if all the objects in the **myList** list are of class **String**, then this list should be created as a **generic collection** using

ArrayList<String> myList = new ArrayList<String>();


## 15.2. Important methods of the ArrayList class : add() , get(), remove(), indexOf(), clear(), size(), isEmpty()


The **add(object)** method adds an object at the end of the list.

The **add(index, object)** method adds an object in the list, at the position given by the index.

The **get(index)** method returns the object found in the list at the position given by the index.

The **remove(index)** method removes the object found in the list at the position given by the index.

The **remove(object)** method removes the object from the list, the first time it is found.

The **indexOf(object)** method returns the index of the object, the first time it is found, or −1 if the object is not found in the list.

The **clear()** method removes all the elements from the list.

The **size()** method returns the number of objects in the list.

The **isEmpty()** method returns **true** when the list is empty, otherwise it returns **false**.

For a list of all the methods of the **ArrayList** class, please go to:

**https://www.javatpoint.com/java-arraylist**


## 15.3. The LinkedList class


The objects in an **LinkedList** are connected like chain links in a chain. In technical terms we say that a **LinkedList** is a **doubly linked list**, that means that each element of the list knows the locations in RAM (the addresses) of its previous element and of its next element. If there is no previous element (it happens for the first element of the list) then the recorded address is NULL. If there is no next element (it happens for the last element of the list) then the recorded address is NULL. The advantage of this implementation is that when an old object is deleted from the list, or when a new object is inserted into the list, all the other objects keep their locations in RAM, and the deletion and insertion operations are very fast. The disadvantage of this implementation is that the objects are less quickly accessed, the Java program has to travel down the list, using the RAM addresses provided by the list elements, until it finds the object it is looking for.

The next program, Java Example 56 , demonstrates how a **LinkedList** is created, populated with objects of type **String**, and how these objects are then listed in order.

By comparing the two programs, Java Example 55 and Java Example 56, one can easily notice that the same **add()**, **get()**, and **remove()** methods are used, and that, from a Java programming point of view, the use of an **ArrayList** list is very similar to the use of a **LinkedList** list. It is only in the machine code implementations and in the RAM allocations that the differences between the two types of list show up.

```java
// Java Example 56
import java.util.LinkedList;
public class Main
{
        public static void main(String[] args)
        {
                LinkedList<String> myList = new LinkedList<String>();
                myList.add("apple");   // the object with index 0
                myList.add("banana");   // the object with index 1
                myList.add("orange");   // the object with index 2
                myList.add("cherry");   // the object with index 3
                myList.add("coconut");   // the object with index 4
                myList.add("pumpkin");   // the object with index 5
                for(int i=0; i<6; i=i+1)
                        System.out.println(myList.get(i));
                myList.remove(4);   // remove the object with index 4, "coconut"
                myList.remove("banana");   // remove the object "banana"
                System.out.println("");
                System.out.println(myList);
                myList.add(2, "cheese");   // add the object "cheese" in the third place
                myList.add(0, "steak");   // add the object "steak" in the first place
                myList.add(6, "ice cream");   // add the object "ice cream" in the last place
                System.out.println("");
                System.out.println(myList);
        }
}
```

**15.4. Important methods of the ArrayList class : add() , get(), remove(), indexOf(), clear(), size(), isEmpty(), addFirst(), addLast(), element(), getFirst(), getLast(), removeFirst(), removeLast(), push(), pop(), peek()**

The **add(object)** method adds an object at the end of the list.

The **add(index, object)** method adds an object in the list, at the position given by the index.

The **get(index)** method returns the object found in the list at the position given by the index.

The **remove(index)** method removes the object found in the list at the position given by the index.

The **remove(object)** method removes the object from the list, the first time it is found.

The **indexOf(object)** method returns the index of the object, the first time it is found, or −1 if the object is not found in the list.

The **clear()** method removes all the elements from the list.

The **size()** method returns the number of objects in the list.

The **isEmpty()** method returns **true** when the list is empty, otherwise it returns **false**.

The **addFirst(object)** method adds an object at the beginning of the list.

The **addLast(object)** method adds an object at the end of the list.

The **element()** method returns the first object in the list.

The **getFirst()** method returns the first object in the list.

The **getLast()** method returns the last object in the list.

The **removeFirst()** method removes the first object in the list.

The **removeLast()** method removes the last object in the list.

The **push(object)** method pushes an object on the stack, that means it adds an object at the top of the list (the top of the stack). A stack is a Last In, First Out (LIFO) list.

The **pop()** method pops an object from the stack, that means it gets, and then it removes, the object from the top of the list (the top of the stack). A stack is a Last In, First Out list.

The **peek()** method peeks at the top object on the stack, that means it gets, but it does not remove, the object from the top of the list (the top of the stack). A stack is a LIFO list.

For a list of all the methods of the **LinkedList** class, please go to:

**https://www.javatpoint.com/java-linkedlist**

The next program, Java Example 57 , demonstrates how a **LinkedList** list is used as a stack.

```java
// Java Example 57
import java.util.LinkedList;
public class Main
{
        public static void main(String[] args)
        {
                String s;
                LinkedList<String> myList = new LinkedList<String>();
                myList.push("apple");
                myList.push("banana");
                myList.push("orange");
                System.out.println(myList);
                s = myList.pop();
                System.out.println(s);   // output : orange
                System.out.println(myList);
                s = myList.peek();
                System.out.println(s);   // output : banana
                System.out.println(myList);
                s = myList.pop();
                System.out.println(s);   // output : banana
                System.out.println(myList);
        }
}
```

## 15.5. Pseudocode methods for collections

The IB booklet "Pseudocode in Examinations" mentions the names of some pseudocode methods used with collections of elements :

The **addItem()** method adds an item (variable, text string, or object) to the collection. Presumably the item is added at the end of the list.

The **getNext()** method gets the next item, without removing it from the collection. This method, the first time when it is called, will return the first item in the collection. Presumably this method uses an index (an integer number) to keep track of the item in focus, the same way a cursor under a letter keeps that letter in focus. After each call, the **getNext()** method increments the index.

The **resetNext()** method resets the index to its smallest value, bringing the first item in the collection in focus.

The **hasNext()** method returns **true** if the index is in the allowed range, this means that the **getNext()** method will read a valid element when called. Otherwise, if all the elements of the collection have been read, and the index is past its largest valid value, the **hasNext()** method returns **false** .

The **isEmpty()** method returns **true** if the collection has no elements, else it returns **false** .

The IB booklet "Pseudocode in Examinations" mentions the names of some methods used with stacks : ( A **stack** is a Last In, First Out (LIFO) list. )

The **push(item)** method pushes an item (variable, text string, or object) on the stack, that means it adds an item at the top of the stack. It is similar to the **addLast(object)** method.

The **pop()** method pops an object from the stack, that means it gets, and then it removes, the object from the top of the stack. It is similar to the **getLast()** method followed by the **removeLast()** method.

The **isEmpty()** method returns **true** when the stack is empty, otherwise it returns **false**.

The IB booklet "Pseudocode in Examinations" mentions the names of some methods used with queues : ( A **queue** is a First In, First Out (FIFO) list. )

The **enqueue(item)** method adds an item (variable, text string, or object) at the end of the queue. It is similar to the **addLast(object)** method.

The **dequeue()** method gets and removes the item from the front of the queue. It is similar to the **getFirst()** method followed by the **removeFirst()** method.

The **isEmpty()** method returns **true** when the queue is empty, otherwise it returns **false**.

While most pseudocode methods are not real Java methods (the exceptions here being **push()** , **pop()** , and **isEmpty()** ), one still needs to know about them because of some questions on the IB Computer Science exam. The students have to be able to read and understand programs written in pseudocode.

Should students also spend time learning how to write programs in pseudocode? The IB booklet "Pseudocode in Examinations"  mentions that "It is accepted that under exam conditions candidates may, in their solutions, use pseudocode similar to a programming language with which they are familiar. This is acceptable. The markscheme will be written using the approved notation. Provided the examiners can see the logic in the candidate's response, regardless of language, it will be credited."

# 16. Random Numbers

Random numbers are very important in computer programming because many video games ( ♠ ♣ ♥ ♦ ) need them. Many computer simulations of real life situations also need them. Java has a few options for generating random numbers: the **Math.random()** method, the **Random** class, and the **shuffle()** method of the **Collections** class.

## 16.1. Generating random numbers using the Math.random() method

The simplest way to generate a random number in Java is to call the **static random()** method of the **Math** class. **Math.random()** returns a real random number (of type **double**) in the [0, 1) interval.

**Math.random()** → real random number in the [0, 1) interval

**MAX*Math.random()** → real random number in the [0, MAX) interval

**MIN + (MAX - MIN)*Math.random()** → real random number in the [MIN, MAX) interval

To change a number of type **double** into a number of type **int** we use the **typecasting operator** **(int)** in front of the numerical expression of type **double**. The real number will be truncated (rounded down) to an integer number, and the fractional part of the real number will be ignored. If N and M are two integer numbers, with $N < M$, then

**N*Math.random()** → real random number in the [0, N) interval

**(int) (N*Math.random())** → integer random number in the $\{0, 1, ... , N - 1\}$ set

**(int) (N*Math.random() + M)** → integer random number in the $\{M, M + 1, ... , M + N - 1\}$ set

---

In particular, to generate an integer random number in the $\{1, 2, 3, 4, 5, 6\}$ set, we use the line:

int i = (int) (6*Math.random() + 1);  // roll of the die

---

Sometimes it is helpful to define a function that generates an integer random number from MIN to MAX, with the limits included. According to the above discussion, $MIN = M$ and $MAX = M + N - 1$. These two equations are equivalent to $M = MIN$ and $N = MAX - MIN + 1$.

**(int) ( (MAX – MIN + 1)*Math.random() + MIN )** → integer random number in the $\{MIN, MIN + 1, ... , MAX - 1, MAX\}$ set

The next program, Java Example 58, prints an integer random number from 1 to 6.

```
// JAVA Example 58
public class Main
{
        public static void main(String[] args)
        {
                int i = (int) (6*Math.random() + 1);   // roll of the die
                System.out.println("roll of the die : i = " + i);
        }
}
```

## 16.2. Generating random numbers using the Random class

An alternative way to generate a random number is to instantiate an object of the **Random** class, and to use one of the **nextInt()** , **nextLong()** , **nextFloat()** , **nextDouble()** , or **nextBoolean()** methods. These methods return random numbers in different intervals.

**nextInt(N)**  →  integer random number in the   $\{0, 1, ... , N-1\}$   set

**nextInt()**  →  integer random number in the   $\{-2^{31}, ... , 2^{31} - 1\}$   set

**nextLong()**  →  long integer random number in the   $\{-2^{63}, ... , 2^{63} - 1\}$   set

**nextFloat()**  →  real random number (of type **float**) in the   $[0, 1)$   interval

**nextDouble()**  →  real random number (of type **double**) in the   $[0, 1)$   interval

**nextBoolean()**  →  random **boolean** value, **true** or **false**

There are two possible ways to use the **nextInt()** method, one with an input argument, and one without. This is an example of **method overloading**.

The next program, Java Example 59, produces random numbers using all these methods of the **Random** class. An objects of the **Random** class needs to be instantiated before these functions are called.

```
// JAVA Example 59
import java.util.Random;
public class Main
{
        public static void main(String[] args)
        {
                Random myRandom = new Random();
                int i = myRandom.nextInt(6) + 1;   // roll of the die
                int j = myRandom.nextInt();
                long k = myRandom.nextLong();
                float f = myRandom.nextFloat();
                double g = myRandom.nextDouble();
                boolean b = myRandom.nextBoolean();
                System.out.println("roll of the die   i = " + i);
                System.out.println("random integer number (int)   j = " + j);
                System.out.println("random integer number (long)   k = " + k);
                System.out.println("random real number (float)   f = " + f);
                System.out.println("random real number (double)   g = " + g);
                System.out.println("random boolean value   b = " + b);
        }
}
```

How do random number generators work? The computer cannot roll a die in order to get a truly random number. The truth is that the "random" numbers produced by the computer are not truly random, they only look like random numbers to an unsuspecting eye. We call them pseudorandom numbers. To generate these pseudorandom numbers the computer starts with a given number, called the seed, and then it applies an algorithm to get the next number in the series. Often the first seed is just the system time in microseconds, or a part of it.

In Java the system time in milliseconds is returned by the **System.currentTimeMillis()** method.

## 16.3. The shuffle() method of the Java Collections class

Another way of introducing randomness into a Java program is to shuffle a collection of objects. This operation is similar to the shuffling of a deck of playing cards. The **shuffle()** method belongs to the **Collections** class, which has a set of **static** methods for storing and manipulating groups of objects. The objects in the collection, like the playing cards in the deck, end up in random positions. The methods of the **Collections** class can act on **ArrayList** or **LinkedList** lists.

The next program, Java Example 60, shuffles a set of 10 integer numbers.

```
// Java Example 60
import java.util.ArrayList;
import java.util.Collections;

public class Main
{
        public static void main(String[] args)
        {
                int N = 10;   // the number of elements in the list
                ArrayList<Integer> myList = new ArrayList<Integer>();
                for(int i=0; i<N; i=i+1) myList.add(i);
                System.out.println("myList before shuffle:");
                for(int i=0; i<N; i=i+1) System.out.println(myList.get(i));
                Collections.shuffle(myList);
                System.out.println("myList after shuffle:");
                for(int i=0; i<N; i=i+1) System.out.println(myList.get(i));
        }
}
```

It is important to notice that the   myList.add(i);   instruction does not add to the collection a primitive variable of type **int**, but instead it adds to the collection an object of class **Integer**. The **Integer** class is one of the so called wrapper classes. The Java wrapper classes transform primitive variables into objects. These objects have just one field variable, the primitive variable we start with, together with some related methods. For example, an object of class **Integer** has just one field variable, a primitive variable of type **long** , packaged together with some helpful methods.

| Primitive variable type | Wrapper class |
|---|---|
| char | Character |
| byte | Byte |
| short | Short |
| long | Integer |
| float | Float |
| double | Double |
| boolean | Boolean |

The wrapper classes can be used with the standard constructor, or with the **autoboxing** feature, which simplifies the conversion of the primitive variable into an object. The **unboxing** feature simplifies the conversion of the object into a primitive variable.

| Standard constructor | With autoboxing | With unboxing |
|---|---|---|
| Character ch = new Character('a'); | Character ch = 'a'; | char c = ch; |
| Byte bt = new Byte((byte) 100); | Byte bt = 100; | byte b = bt; |
| Short st = new Short((short) 30000); | Short st = 30000; | short s = st; |
| Integer it = new Integer(1000000); | Integer it = 1000000; | long i = it; |
| Float ft = new Float(3.1416); | Float ft = 3.1416F; | float f = ft; |
| Double db = new Double(5.6E40); | Double db = 5.6E40; | double d = db; |
| Boolean bn = new Boolean(true); | Boolean bn = true; | boolean b = bn; |

## 16.4. Important static methods of the Java wrapper classes

Each wrapper class comes with some **static** methods. Two of the most commonly used methods turn a **String** object into a primitive variable, and vice-versa. The **Integer.parseInt(String s)** method returns an integer ( **int** ) number. The **String** object **s** is converted into the **int** equivalent. For example **Integer.parseInt("–505")** returns –505 . The **Integer.toString(int)** method returns a **String** object, the equivalent of the integer number. For example **Integer.toString(505)** returns **"505"** . There is also a **toString()** method that does not have an **int** parameter, used with objects that have been initialized.

| Conversion from String | Conversion to String |
|---|---|
| **Warning!** **Character.parseChar()** does not exist. | String s = Character.toString('a'); |
| byte b = Byte.parseByte("100"); | String s = Byte.toString((byte) 100); |
| short s = Short.parseShort("30000"); | String s = Short.toString((short) 30000); |
| int i = Integer.parseInt("1000000"); | String s = Integer.toString(1000000); |
| float f = Float.parseFloat("3.1416"); | String s = Float.toString(3.1416F); |
| double d = Double.parseDouble("5.6E40"); | String s = Double.toString(5.6E40); |
| boolean t = Boolean.parseBoolean("true"); | String s = Boolean.toString(true); |

## 17. Object-Oriented Programming: Encapsulation


### 17.1. Accessor (getter) and mutator (setter) methods


Encapsulation is a fundamental feature of Object-Oriented Programming. A capsule, in general, is a small container with some protected content inside. Think about a pharmaceutical capsule (a small gelatinous case holding the medication), a space capsule (a small spacecraft protecting the astronauts during landing), or a time capsule (a sealed box with some objects intentionally saved for future times).

In Java encapsulation describes the protection of some instance variables inside an object.

In Java encapsulation is implemented using the **private** keyword in front of the protected instance variables (field variables). As a consequence these protected field variables can be accessed (read or written) only by methods of the same object. Usually the objects have dedicated **public** methods that read from RAM the value of the **private** instance variables, called accessor methods (also called getter methods), and dedicated methods that write into RAM the value of the **private** instance variables, called mutator methods (also called setter methods). (How to remember the "mutator" name? Think that in biology a mutation is a change in the DNA. A mutator method brings a change of value.)

The biggest advantage of encapsulation is that the protected instance variables are safe from unauthorized direct access. Indirect access is still granted through the **public** accessor (getter) and mutator (setter) methods, or through other **public** methods of that class. Encapsulation also minimizes the chance of an accidental corruption of the data, since in minimizes the chance of a programming error with that effect. Encapsulation is a form of abstraction, it hides from the user the implementation details of the accessor and mutator methods. As a result the maintenance and/or the modification of the accessor and mutator methods is done easier, without the need of making any changes in the classes that are accessing (reading or writing) the protected instance variables.

You have already seen an example of encapsulation in Java Example 36. In that program the **private myText** text string is set by the **MyHello()** constructor and then is printed out by the **printGreeting()** function. We now expand the Java Example 36 program by adding accessor (getter) and mutator (setter) methods.


The program shown in Java Example 61 has two classes. The **public Main** class has the **static main()** method, which is the entry point into the program. The **MyHello** class has one instance variable, the **private myText** text string object. This **private** instance variable can be read or written only by the four **public** methods of the **MyHello** class: **MyHello()** , **printGreeting()** , **setText()** , and **getText()** .

The **greeting** object is declared and created (instantiated) in the first line of the **main()** method. The **greeting.myText** instance variable is given the initial value of "Hello World!" by the **MyHello()** constructor. This initial value is printed on the screen by the **printGreeting()** method. Next, the initial value of **greeting.myText** is changed into "I love Computer Science!" by the **setText()** mutator method. This new value of **greeting.myText** is read by the **getText()** accessor method, which returns the value of this **private** text string. The new message is then printed on the screen by the **System.out.println()** method.

```java
// Java Example 61
public class Main
{
        public static void main(String[] args)
        {
                MyHello greeting = new MyHello("Hello World!");
                greeting.printGreeting();
                greeting.setText("I love Computer Science!");
                String newText = greeting.getText();
                System.out.println(newText);
        }
}

class MyHello
{
        private String myText;   // the protected instance variable

        public MyHello(String text)   // the constructor
        {
                myText = text;
        }

        public void printGreeting()
        {
                System.out.println(myText);
        }

        public void setText(String text)   // the mutator (setter) method
        {
                myText = text;
        }

        public String getText()   // the accessor (getter) method
        {
                return myText;
        }
}
```

## 17.2. The JAVA access modifiers: public, private, protected

To **access a variable** means that you can find (read, get) or change (write, set) its value.

To **access a function** means that you can use (call, execute, invoke) that function.

To **access an object** means that you can access the variables, functions, and objects that belong to that given object.

A JAVA **access modifier** is a JAVA keyword that determines what functions have or do not have access to the variables, functions, or objects to whom that JAVA access modifier applies.

The operational definitions of the Java access modifiers are given in the table below:

| none (default) | The variables, functions, and objects from that given class can be accessed by functions from classes in **the same package** . |
| public | The variables, functions, and objects from that given class can be accessed by functions from **any class** (from any package). |
| private | The variables, functions, and objects from that given class can be accessed by functions from **the same class** . Functions from other classes in the same package do not have access. |
| protected | The variables, functions, and objects from that given class can be accessed by functions from **the same class** or from **any of its subclasses** . Functions from other classes in **the same package** also have access. |

A summary of the consequences of the Java access modifiers is given in the table below:

| Access modifier | Access by functions from the same class | Access by functions from the same package | Access by functions from subclasses of other packages | Access by functions from any class (from any package) |
| --- | --- | --- | --- | --- |
| public | Yes | Yes | Yes | Yes |
| protected | Yes | Yes | Yes | No |
| none (default) | Yes | Yes | No | No |
| private | Yes | No | No | No |

One question still remains. What is a subclass? Read the next chapter to find the answer.

# 18. Object-Oriented Programming: Inheritance

Inheritance is a fundamental feature of Object-Oriented Programming. Inheritance, in general, refers to the transfer of some property (money, houses, valuable objects) from a dead person to his or her children, other family members, or friends.

In Java **inheritance** describes the transfer, from one class (**the parent class**) to another class (**the child class**), of all the non-private field variables, methods, and classes of the parent class.

The parent class is also called **the superclass**, or **the base class**. The child class is also called the **subclass**, or **the derived class**. The child class does not inherit the constructor(s) of the parent class, but the default constructor of the child class always starts by calling the default constructor of the parent class. (Not needed for the IB CS exam: A constructor of the child class can call a constructor of the parent class using the **super()** keyword.)

In Java inheritance is implemented using the **extends** keyword in the declaration of the child class. The parent class must be declared in the Java program before the child class is declared.

**class ParentClass { ... }**

**class ChildClass extends ParentClass { ... }**

In this way an object of type **ChildClass** will have all the non-private field variables, methods, and objects of an object of type **ParentClass** . The **ChildClass** class can also have additional field variables, methods, and objects, which the **ParentClass** class does not have.

The biggest advantage of inheritance is the ability of the child class to reuse code written for the parent class. Inheritance not only shortens the development time of a new program, but also results in better structured and more robust programs, since usually the code of the parent class has been optimized and is well tested against all kinds of possible errors.

The program shown in Java Example 62 has three classes. The **public Main** class has the **static main()** method, which is the entry point into the program. The **Book** parent class (superclass) has two field variables, **title** and **author** , and one method, **printInfo()** . The **Textbook** child class (subclass) has an additional field variable, **subject** , and an additional method, **printMoreInfo()** . The **myTextbook** object, which is an instance of the **Textbook** child class, has the three field variables and the two methods listed above. After the **myTextbook** object is created (instantiated), all its field variables are given values, and all its methods are called from the **main()** method. There is no distinction between field variables and methods that are inherited, and field variables and methods that are not inherited. They all work in the same way, as if all the Java lines of code from the body of the **Book** parent class were copied and pasted inside the body of the **Textbook** child class.

```java
// Java Example 62
public class Main
{

        public static void main(String[] args)
        {

                Textbook myTextbook = new Textbook();
                myTextbook.title = "Elements";
                myTextbook.author = "Euclid";
                myTextbook.subject = "Geometry";
                myTextbook.printInfo();
                myTextbook.printMoreInfo();

        }

}


class Book   // the parent class
{

        String title;
        String author;

        void printInfo()
        {

                System.out.println("title = " + title);
                System.out.println("author = " + author);

        }


}


class Textbook extends Book   // the child class
{

        String subject;

        void printMoreInfo()
        {

                System.out.println("subject = " + subject);

        }

}
```

Sometimes the child class will define a field variable that has the same name as a field variable of the parent class. In this situation, inside the body of the child class, the child variable will replace the parent variable, because the definition of the child variable is inside the curly brackets { } of the child class, and thus it has priority there. More clarity can be achieved by using the **this** keyword, which, inside the body of the child class, refers to the current object. The instance variable of the parent class is still available, using the **super** keyword, which, inside the body of the child class, refers to the parent class.

The next program, Java Example 63, shows how to access field variables that have the same name in both the child and the parent classes. The program demonstrates the use of the **this** and **super** keywords. The **myBook** object of class **Book** is the parent, and the **myTextbook** object of class **Textbook** is the child. The two field variables are named **myBook.title** and **myTextbook.title** . From within the **myTextbook** object, **title** and **this.title** refer to **myTextbook.title** , but **super.title** refers to an inherited field variable identical to **myBook.title** . This inherited field variable exists even without an instantiated **myBook** object.

```java
// Java Example 63
public class Main
{
        public static void main(String[] args)
        {
                Book myBook = new Book();
                System.out.println(myBook.title);   // output : How to win at poker
                Textbook myTextbook = new Textbook();
                System.out.println(myTextbook.title);   // output : Applied statistics
                myTextbook.printDemo();
        }
}


class Book   // the parent class
{
        String title = "How to win at poker";

}


class Textbook extends Book   // the child class
{
        String title = "Applied statistics";

        void printDemo()
        {
                System.out.println(title);   // output : Applied statistics
                System.out.println(this.title);   // output : Applied statistics
                System.out.println(super.title);   // output : How to win at poker

        }

}
```

Sometimes the child class will define a method that has the same name and the same signature (the same return type and the same input parameters) as a method of the parent class. This is called method overriding. In this situation, inside the body of the child class, the child method will replace the parent method, because the definition of the child method is inside the curly brackets { } of the child class, and thus it has priority there. More clarity can be achieved by using the **this** keyword, which, inside the body of the child class, refers to the current object. The method of the parent class is still available, using the **super** keyword, which, inside the body of the child class, refers to the parent class.

The next program, Java Example 64, shows how to access methods that have the same name in both the child and the parent classes. The program demonstrates the use of the **this** and **super** keywords. The **myBook** object of class **Book** is the parent, and the **myTextbook** object of class **Textbook** is the child. The two methods are named **myBook.printTitle()** and **myTextbook.printTitle()** . From within the **myTextbook** object, **printTitle()** and **this.printTitle()** refer to **myTextbook.printTitle()** , but **super.printTitle()** refers to an inherited method identical to **myBook.printTitle()** . This inherited method exists even without an instantiated **myBook** object.

```java
// Java Example 64
public class Main
{
        public static void main(String[] args)
        {
                Book myBook = new Book();
                myBook.printTitle();   // output : How to win at poker
                Textbook myTextbook = new Textbook();
                myTextbook.printTitle();   // output : Applied statistics
                myTextbook.printDemo();
        }
}

class Book   // the parent class
{
        void printTitle()
        {
        System.out.println("How to win at poker");
        }
}

class Textbook extends Book   // the child class
{
        void printTitle()
        {
                System.out.println("Applied statistics");
        }

        void printDemo()
        {
                printTitle();   // output : Applied statistics
                this.printTitle();   // output : Applied statistics
                super.printTitle();   // output : How to win at poker
        }
}
```

# 19. Object-Oriented Programming: Polymorphism

Polymorphism is a fundamental feature of Object-Oriented Programming. In Greek "polys" means "many" or "much" and "morphe" means "form" or "shape". In general polymorphism refers to a situation in which something has several different shapes, forms, behaviors, etc.

> In Java polymorphism describes a situation in which a unique method name is associated with several different behaviors. If we identify a method not by its name, but by its body (the code), then polymorphism means that we can have different methods with the same name.

In Java there are two types of polymorphism: compile time polymorphism (due to method overloading) and run time polymorphism (due to method overriding).

## 19.1. Method overloading (compile time polymorphism)

In Java the same class can have two or more different methods with the same name, but with different numbers or types of input parameters. This is called method overloading. Java decides which method to call (to use) when the program is compiled, based on the number or the types of the input variables. The number of input parameters of a function, together with the type (primitive variable type or class type) of each of these input parameters, is called the signature of the function.

> Warning! One should also remember that the type of the output variable (the return type of a function) cannot be used in Java to distinguish between two functions (two methods) with the same name and with the same signature (the same number and the same type of input parameters).

Not only methods (functions) can show polymorphism, arithmetic operators can also have polymorphic behavior. The "+" addition operator can add two numbers, or concatenate two text strings. The "/" division operator can divide two real numbers (with no rounding of the answer), or divide two integer numbers (with the rounding down of the answer to an integer value).

The next program, Java Example 65, demonstrates the polymorphic behavior of the division operator.

```
// Java Example 65
public class Main
{
        public static void main(String[] args)
        {
                System.out.println(" 12 / 5 = " + 12/5);   // output : 2
                System.out.println(" 12.0 / 5.0 = " + 12.0/5.0);   // output : 2.4
        }
}
```

The next program, Java Example 66, uses the **vectorLength()** method to calculate the length (the magnitude) of a vector. There are four different implementations of the method, all with the same name, but each with different numbers of input parameters. This is a case of method overloading. We have a **vectorLength()** implementation for one dimensional vectors, another one for two dimensional vectors, another one for three dimensional vectors, and another one for four dimensional vectors. The length of the vector is calculated using the **Math.sqrt()** square root function, available in Java as a **static** method of the **Math** class. To optimize the program, just for the one dimensional case, one could also use the **Math.abs(x)** absolute value function instead of the **Math.sqrt(x\*x)** square root function.

```java
// Java Example 66
public class Main
{
        public static void main(String[] args)
        {
                System.out.println( "length of (-7) = " + vectorLength(-7) );
                System.out.println( "length of (3, 4) = " + vectorLength(3, 4) );
                System.out.println( "length of (3, 4, 12) = " + vectorLength(3, 4, 12) );
                System.out.println( "length of (3, 4, 12, -17) = " + vectorLength(3, 4, 12, -17) );
        }

        static double vectorLength(double x)
        {
                return Math.sqrt(x*x);
        }

        static double vectorLength(double x, double y)
        {
                return Math.sqrt(x*x + y*y);
        }

        static double vectorLength(double x, double y, double z)
        {
                return Math.sqrt(x*x + y*y + z*z);
        }

        static double vectorLength(double x, double y, double z, double u)
        {
                return Math.sqrt(x*x + y*y + z*z + u*u);
        }
}
```

The next program, Java Example 67, gives another example of method overloading. Here the **sum()** function can add 2 integer numbers (of type **int**), 3 integer numbers, or 2 real numbers (of type **double**). The different implementations of the **sum()** method have either different numbers of input parameters (2 or 3) or different types of input parameters ( **int** or **double** ).

What happens if we call the **sum()** function with two non-matching input arguments, one integer number and one real number? Will the first or the third implementation be used, or will we get an error message? Run the program and discover that in this case the third implementation of the **sum()** method is used. It turns out that in a situation like this Java changes a number of type **int** into a number of type **double** . This happens because there is no loss of precision when an integer number is converted into a real number. The opposite is not true, usually there is some rounding up or rounding down when a real number is converted into an integer number.

```java
// Java Example 67
public class Main
{
        public static void main(String[] args)
        {
                System.out.println("1 + 8 = " + sum(1, 8));
                System.out.println("2 + 3 + 4 = " + sum(2, 3, 4));
                System.out.println("4.0 + 5.0 = " + sum(4.0, 5.0));
                System.out.println("3 + 6.0 = " + sum(3, 6.0));
        }

        static int sum(int x, int y)
        {
                System.out.println("the first implementation of the method sum()");
                return x + y;
        }

        static int sum(int x, int y, int z)
        {
                System.out.println("the second implementation of the method sum()");
                return x + y + z;
        }

        static double sum(double x, double y)
        {
                System.out.println("the third implementation of the method sum()");
                return x + y;
        }
}
```

## 19.2. Method overriding (run time polymorphism)

In Java a parent class (a superclass) and a child class (a subclass) can have different methods with the same name and with the same **signature** (the same number and the same types of input parameters). This is called **method overriding**.

In Java, according to inheritance rules, an object of a child class is also an object of the parent class (this is the IS-A relationship). As a result, one can instantiate (create) an object of a child class that has an object reference (a pointer) of the parent class type. In other words, a constructor of a child class can be called to instantiate an object of the parent class. The object is of the parent class type because it was declared in this way, and the constructor of a child class cannot change this declaration statement.

An object of the parent class can be instantiated (created) using a constructor of a child class.

**Warning!** When an object of the parent class (an object that has an object reference of parent class type) is instantiated using a constructor of a child class, the object can access only the field variables and the methods of the parent class.

**Warning!** Please also notice that, because an object of the parent class is not an object of a child class, one cannot call the constructor of the parent class in order to instantiate an object of a child class.

The next program, Java Example 68, shows how a constructor of the child class can be used to instantiate an object of the parent class. For comparison, the other two more common options (when the constructor matches the class of the declared object) are also shown.

```java
// Java Example 68
public class Main
{
        public static void main(String[] args)
        {
                Book myBook = new Book();
                Textbook myTextbook = new Textbook();
                Book trouble = new Textbook();   // a Textbook object IS-A Book object
                // Textbook impossible = new Book();   // error message
        }
}

class Book   // the parent class
{
        String title = "How to win at poker";
}

class Textbook extends Book   // the child class
{
        String title = "Applied statistics";
}
```

Suppose that we have a parent class, a child class, and method overriding. During compile time, based only on the object reference (known to be of parent class type), Java cannot decide which method to use, the one of the parent class or the one of the child class. This is because the Java compiler cannot tell, based on just the object reference of parent class type, whether the parent class constructor was used, or whether a child class constructor was used when the object was instantiated (created). Java will decide which method to call only when the program is running, based on the class type of the actual object associated with the method call, at that specific time and place in the program.

The same object reference (of parent class type) can point to a parent object in one place in the program, and to a child object in a different place in the program.

In the next program, Java Example 69, the **myPet** object reference (of class **Animal**) can hold the address of an object of class **Animal** (the parent class) or the address of an object of class **Dog** (the child class). The **Animal** parent class (the superclass) has a method named **talk()** that is overridden by the **Dog** child class (the subclass). In the Java program the two   myPet.talk();   lines of code, although identical, will print different messages.  A human looking at the Java program listed below can tell right away what **talk()** method will be called by each   myPet.talk();   instruction, but the Java compiler, who works with only one instruction at a time, cannot. The Java compiler cannot mentally go through the listing of the program, line by line, and then make decisions based on past instructions.

```
Java Example 69
public class Main
{
        public static void main(String[] args)
        {
                Animal myPet;
                myPet = new Animal();
                myPet.talk();   // output : I am an animal.
                myPet = new Dog();
                myPet.talk();   // output : I am a dog.
        }
}


class Animal
{
        void talk()
        {
                System.out.println("I am an animal.");
        }
}

class Dog extends Animal
{
        void talk()
        {
                System.out.println("I am a dog.");
        }
}
```

The same object reference (of parent class type) can point to a parent object, or to a child object, at the same place in the program. Such a circumstance makes it easy to understand why Java can decide what method to call only at run time, and not at compile time.

In the next program, Java Example 70, the **myPet** object reference (of class **Animal)** can hold the address of an object of class **Animal** (the parent class) or the address of an object of class **Dog** (the child class). The **Animal** parent class (the superclass) has a method named **talk()** that is overridden by the **Dog** child class (the subclass). A random number decides the actual class of the instantiated **myPet** object, and it is impossible to know at compile time what **talk()** method will be called by the myPet.talk();   instruction at run time. Run the program several times to see that different messages are indeed printed by the one and only  myPet.talk();   instruction.

```
Java Example 70
public class Main
{
        public static void main(String[] args)
        {
                Animal myPet;
                if(Math.random() < 0.5)
                {
                        myPet = new Animal();
                }
                else
                {
                        myPet = new Dog();
                }
                myPet.talk();   // which method to call can be decided only at run time
        }
}

class Animal
{
        void talk()
        {
                System.out.println("I am an animal.");
        }
}

class Dog extends Animal
{
        void talk()
        {
                System.out.println("I am a dog.");
        }
}
```

# 20. The relationships between Java classes, and their UML diagrams

There are three possible ways in which two classes can be related to each other. These three connections between classes are described as inheritance, aggregation, and dependency.

## 20.1. The "IS A" relationship (inheritance)

The inheritance relationship describes two classes related by inheritance, for example:

**class ParentClass { ... }**

**class ChildClass extends ParentClass { ... }**

The child class inherits all the non-private instance variables, methods, and objects of the parent class. Looking at just these inherited properties, there is no difference between the two classes. We say that an object of type **ChildClass** is also an object of type **ParentClass** . From a practical point of view, the programmer needs to be aware of the fact that any changes in the declarations and definitions of the parent class will also be inherited by the child class.

## 20.2. The "HAS A" relationship (aggregation)

The aggregation relationship describes two classes, when an object of one class type owns an object (or an array of objects) of the other class type. For example:

**class Book { ... }**

**class BookShelf { Book bestBook; Book [] myBooks; ... }**

We say that an object of type **BookShelf** has objects of type **Book** . From a practical point of view, the programmer needs to be aware of the fact that changes in the declarations and definitions of the **Book** class will probably require changes in the code of the **BookShelf** class.

## 20.3. The "USES A" relationship (dependency)

The dependency relationship describes two connected classes, when an object of one class uses a field variable or a method of another class. For example, we could have an object of a given class (or a method of a **static** class) that gets a random number using the **Math** class, with the help of the **Math.random()** method. In this case that given class (or maybe the **static Main()** class that does not need an instantiated object) uses the **Math** class.

It is good programming practice to reduce the number of relationships between classes, whenever this is possible. The more connections between classes and their instantiated objects we have, the harder it is to make changes to the Java program, because the changes have to be implemented simultaneously in several different places. More connections between classes also make a Java program harder to read and understand. The extra effort to read, understand, use, and/or modify a program is described as increased maintenance overhead.

The next program, Java Example 71, has five classes: **Main** , **Parent** , **Child** , **Dog** , and **Vet** . The **Main** class HAS AN object of the **Child** class and USES the **Vet** class in a direct way. The instantiated **myChild** object is a **Child** (an object of the **Child** class), but because of inheritance it IS A **Parent** (an object of the **Parent** class) as well. An instantiated object of the **Child** class HAS AN instantiated object of the **Dog** class. In this case the **myChild** object HAS the **myDog** object.

```java
// Java Example 71
public class Main
{
        public static void main(String[] args)
        {
                Child myChild = new Child();
                myChild.firstName = "Peter";
                myChild.lastName = "Thompson";
                myChild.myDog.name = "Lassie";
                Vet.vaccinate(myChild.myDog);
        }
}

class Parent
{
        String firstName;
        String lastName;
}

class Child extends Parent
{
        Dog myDog = new Dog();
}

class Dog
{
        String name;
        boolean vaccinated;
}

class Vet
{
        static void vaccinate(Dog aDog)
        {
                aDog.vaccinated = true;
        }
}
```

Each Java class can be represented with the help of a Unified Modeling Language (UML) diagram, and the relationships between the Java classes can also be represented using these UML diagrams.

A UML class diagram has three layers. On top we have the name of the class. In the middle we have the field variables (primitive variables or objects) of the class, and on the bottom we have the methods of the class. When the field variables or methods are **private**, we put a minus (-) sign in front. When the field variables or methods are **public**, we put a plus (+) sign in front. The type (variable type or class) of the field variables must follow their names. The return type of the methods must follow their names.

An example of a UML diagram is given below, for a class named **Library** .

| Library |
| --- |
| + numberOfBooks : int |
| + addressOfLibrary : String |
| - books : Book[] |
| + borrowBook(Book) : void |
| + returnBook(Book) : void |
| + isAvailable(Book) : boolean |

The relationships between the Java classes from the Java Example 71 program can be represented using UML diagrams in this way:

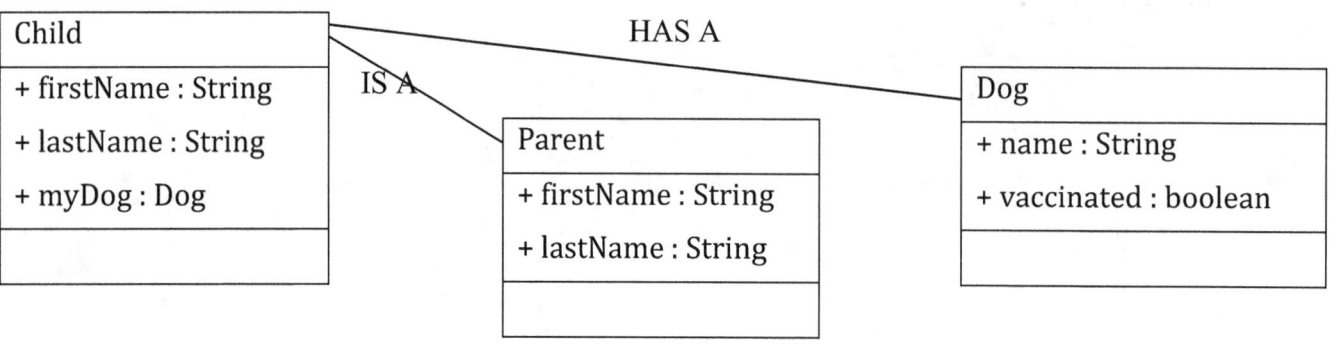

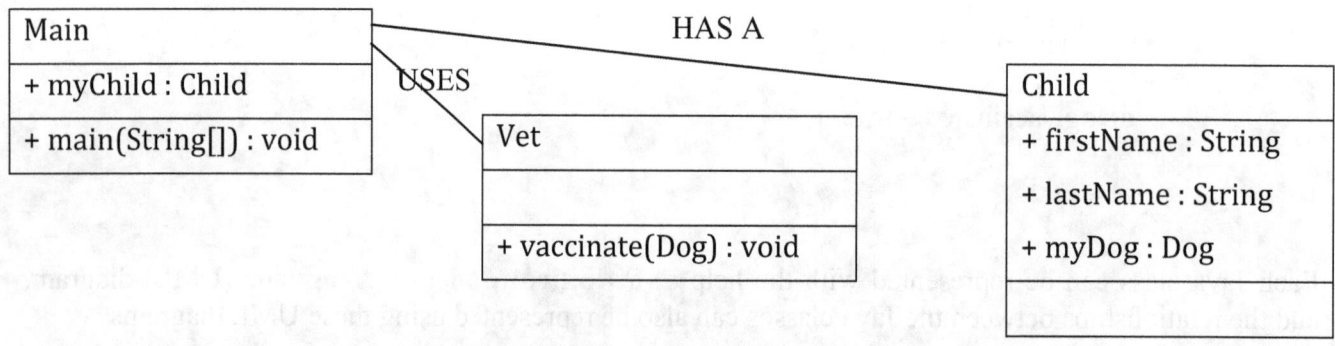

## 21. Reading from and writing into text files

In a text file every line ends with a special End Of Line (EOL) character (or sequence of characters), and the text file itself ends with a special End Of File (EOF) character. These special characters depend on the operating system running on the computer.

### 21.1. Reading from a text file in sequential order

Reading from text files is done with the help of objects of type (class) **File** , **FileReader** , and **BufferedReader** .

The **File(String pathname)** constructor creates a **File** object from a path name. The path name specifies the directory and the file name. An example of a path name is "C:\TextFiles\abc.txt". The **File** class has basic methods for creating new files and directories, searching for files and directories, finding some file properties (readable, writable, length, etc.), and deleting files and directories. The **boolean exists()** method will return **true** when the file or directory already exists. The **boolean createNewFile()** method will return **true** when the new file is successfully created. The **boolean mkdir()** method will return **true** when the new directory is successfully created. The **boolean delete()** method will return **true** when the file or directory is successfully deleted. A directory must be empty before it can be deleted. These methods will throw an **IOException** whenever the operating system reports an error.

The **FileReader(File myFile)** constructor creates a **FileReader** object from a **File** object. The **FileReader** class has methods that will read alphanumeric characters from a text file. The **int read()** method will read one character, which is the return value of this function. The **int read(char [] c, int offset, int len)** method will read a sequence of characters, placing them into an array. These methods will throw an **IOException** whenever there is an error.

The **BufferedReader(FileReader myFileReader)** constructor creates a **BufferedReader** object from a **FileReader** object. Reading alphanumeric characters from a text file, without a buffer, is not very efficient, because the text file on the hard disk is accessed for each reading operation, and this is a relatively slow process. To improve performance the **BufferedReader** object uses an input buffer (a space in RAM) of specified or of default size, where it loads big chunks of information from the text file. In addition to the **int read()** methods, the **BufferedReader** class has a **String readLine()** method that will read a line of text from a stream of characters. The line of text is the return value of this function. When there are no more lines to read from a text file, the return value is **null** . The **void close()** method will close the source (the stream) of alphanumeric information and will release any system resources associated with it. The **BufferedReader** class also has a **boolean ready()** method, used to prevent errors during a function call of **read()** , something that could happen whenever the stream of alphanumeric characters is not ready (for example, during online communication).

> Warning! The **readLine()** method will crash when the stream of characters does not end with EOL or EOF, even when the return value from **ready()** is **true** .

Because of all the methods that may throw an **IOException** during the process of reading from a text file, the Java code has to be written inside a try - catch block. It looks like this:

**try { instructions;**

**} catch (IOException e) { System.out.println( e.getMessage() ); }**

The **getMessage()** method of the **IOException** class will print the appropriate error message.

The next program, Java Example 72, reads all the lines of text from a text file, and prints them on the screen. The program also counts how many lines of text the given file has.

Step 1. Go to the root of your hard disk (**C:\**) and create a new folder. Right-click with the mouse, then select **New|Folder** . Change the name of the folder from **New folder** to **JavaTextFiles** .

Step 2. Inside the **JavaTextFiles** folder create a new text file. Right-click with the mouse, then select **New|Text Document**. Change the name of the file from **New Text Document.txt** to **text_file_1.txt** .

Step 3. Using **Notepad**, open the **text_file_1.txt** file, type the five lines of text shown below, and then save the text file and close Notepad. The text file should look like this:

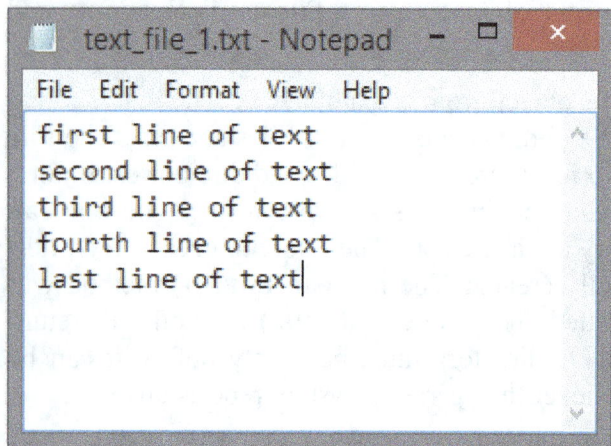

Step 4. Double click on the NetBeans shortcut link on the desktop.

Step 5. From the menu select **File|New Project...** or click on the **New Project** button.

Step 6. In the **New Project** window the **Java Application** option should be already selected. Click on the **Next** button.

Step 7. In the **New Java Application** window type the **TextFileRead** project name. The **Create Main Class** checkbox should be checked. Click on the **Finish** button.

Step 8. Delete all the comments that were automatically included in the Java program, and align the curly braces on the left side.

Step 9. Type the Java Example 72 program, which is listed on the next page.

Step 10. Click on the Save All button.

Step 11. Click on the Run Project button.

A successful execution of the Java Example 72 program will produce this output:

```
Variables    Output - TextFileRead (run)  ×
    run:
    The data stream is ready.
    the first character is : f
    line 1 is : irst line of text
    line 2 is : second line of text
    line 3 is : third line of text
    line 4 is : fourth line of text
    line 5 is : last line of text
    The text file has 5 lines of text.
    BUILD SUCCESSFUL (total time: 0 seconds)
```

Please notice that once an alphanumeric character has been read using the **read()** method, it will not be read again by a subsequent use of the **readLine()** method.


```java
// Java Example 72
package textfileread;
import java.io.File;
import java.io.IOException;
import java.io.FileReader;
import java.io.BufferedReader;

public class TextFileRead
{
        public static void main(String[] args)
        {
                try   // reading lines from a text file
                {
                        File myFile = new File("C:/JavaTextFiles/text_file_1.txt");
                        FileReader fr = new FileReader(myFile);
                        BufferedReader br = new BufferedReader(fr);
                        if (br.ready()) System.out.println("The data stream is ready.");
                        int data = br.read();
                        System.out.println("the first character is : " + (char) data);
                        int n = 0; // the number of text lines in the text file
                        String textLine = br.readLine();
                        while (textLine != null)
                        {
                                n = n + 1;
                                System.out.println("line " + n + " is : " + textLine);
                                textLine = br.readLine();
                        }
                        br.close();
                        System.out.println("The text file has " + n + " lines of text.");
                } catch (IOException e) { System.out.println( e.getMessage() ); }
        }
}
```

A shorter version of this program does not use the **myFile** object of class **File** , but instead uses the one-line expression   FileReader fr = new FileReader("C:/JavaTextFiles/text_file_1.txt");

The next program, Java Example 73, creates a new text file. The program uses two important methods of the **File** class, the **exists()** method and the **createNewFile()** method.

Start NetBeans, as with the previous program, and in the **New Java Application** window type the **TextFileCreate** project name. Type the Java Example 73 program, save the source file, and run the project. Verify that an empty file named **text_file_2.txt** has been created in the **C:/JavaTextFiles** directory. Run the program again. The first time that you run the program you should get the message "The file has been successfully created." . The second time that you run the program you should get the message "The file is already present there." .

```java
// Java Example 73
package textfilecreate;
import java.io.File;
import java.io.IOException;

public class TextFileCreate
{
      public static void main(String[] args)
      {
            try   // create a new text file
            {
                  File myFile = new File("C:/JavaTextFiles/text_file_2.txt");
                  if(myFile.exists())
                  {
                        System.out.println("The file is already present there.");
                  }
                  else
                  {
                        boolean fvar = myFile.createNewFile();
                        if (fvar)
                        {
                           System.out.println("The file has been successfully created.");
                        }
                        else
                        {
                           System.out.println("ERROR: The file has not been created.");
                        }
                  }
            } catch (IOException e) { System.out.println( e.getMessage() ); }
      }
}
```

The **File** class has other important methods, for example : **isDirectory()** , **isFile()** , **delete()** , **mkdir()** , **renameTo()** , **setReadOnly()** . For a list of all the methods of the **File** class, please go to :
**https://www.tutorialspoint.com/java/java_file_class.htm**

## 21.2. Writing into a text file in sequential order

Writing into text files is done with the help of objects of type (class) **File** , **FileWriter** , **BufferedWriter** , and **PrintWriter** .

The **File(String pathname)** constructor creates a **File** object from a path name. The path name specifies the directory and the file name. An example of a path name is "C:\TextFiles\abc.txt".

The **FileWriter(File myFile)** constructor creates a **FileWriter** object from a **File** object. If the text file with the given path name does not exist, then this constructor will create it.

> **Warning!** If the text file with the given path name exists, then this constructor will erase all the previous information stored in the text file. In order to save the old information, and append the new information (add the new information at the end of the existing text file), we have to use the **FileWriter(File myFile, true)** constructor.

The **FileWriter** class has methods that will write alphanumeric characters into a text file. The **public void write()** method will write only one alphanumeric character. The **public void write(char [] c)** method will write a sequence of characters, as given in an array. The **public void write(String text)** method will write a text string. These methods will throw an **IOException** whenever there is an error.

The **BufferedWriter(FileWriter myFileWriter)** constructor creates a **BufferedWriter** object from a **FileWriter** object. Writing alphanumeric characters into a text file, without a buffer, is not very efficient, because the text file on the hard disk is accessed for each writing operation, and this is a relatively slow process. To improve performance the **BufferedWriter** object uses an output buffer (a space in RAM) of specified or of default size, where it saves information that is waiting to be written into the text file. In addition to the **write()** methods, the **BufferedWriter** class has a **void newLine()** method that will write a line separator (an EOL code). The **void close()** method will flush the buffer (that means it will write all of the updated information into the text file), close the text file, and then release any system resources associated with it.

The **PrintWriter(BufferedWriter myBufferedWriter)** constructor creates a **PrintWriter** object from a **BufferedWriter** object. In addition to the well-known **print()** and **println()** methods, the **PrintWriter** class has a very useful **printf()** method that prints formatted output. ( We can also get formatted output with the **System.out.printf()** or with the **String.format()** methods. ) What is the meaning of "formatted output"? Special symbols are used inside a text string. These symbols act as placeholders for variables of various types, describing the type of variable, the total number of characters, the number of decimal places, and other formatting details. The general syntax of the format specifiers is **% [flag][width][.precision] conv_character** The special symbols (conversion characters) for formatted output are:

**%d** = decimal integer number ( Example: %5d for a number written with 5 characters )

**%f** = floating point number ( Example: %6.2f for a number written with 6 characters, including the decimal point, and 2 decimal places )

**%c** = alphanumeric character ( **%C** = alphanumeric character with uppercase letter )

**%s** = text string ( **%S** = text string with uppercase letters )

**%h** = hashcode ( A hashcode is a Java identifier derived from a RAM address. )

**%n** = new line

Because of all the methods that may throw an **IOException** during the process of writing into a text file, the Java code has to be written inside a try - catch block.

The next program, Java Example 74, creates a new text file called "text_file_3.txt", and writes (appends) a few lines of text into this file using the **write()** , **newLine()** , **print()** , **println()** , and **printf()** methods.

Start NetBeans, as with the previous program, and in the **New Java Application** window type the **TextFileWrite** project name. Type the program, save the source file, and run the project. Verify that a text file named **text_file_3.txt** has been created in the **C:/JavaTextFiles** directory. Open the **text_file_3.txt** file and verify that it has four lines of text. Close the text file. Run the program again. Open the **text_file_3.txt** file again and verify that four more lines of text, identical to the first four, have been added to the old content.

```java
// Java Example 74
package textfilewrite;
import java.io.File;
import java.io.IOException;
import java.io.FileWriter;
import java.io.BufferedWriter;
import java.io.PrintWriter;

public class TextFileWrite
{
        public static void main(String[] args)
        {
                try   // write inside an existing text file
                {
                        File myFile = new File("C:/JavaTextFiles/text_file_3.txt");
                        FileWriter fw = new FileWriter(myFile, true);   // append
                        BufferedWriter bw = new BufferedWriter(fw);
                        bw.write("first line of text");
                        bw.newLine();
                        PrintWriter pw = new PrintWriter(bw);
                        pw.print("second line of text");
                        pw.println();
                        pw.println("third line of text");
                        pw.printf("%d + %d = %d %n", 2, 3, 5);
                        pw.close();
                        System.out.println("Text lines written successfully.");
                } catch (IOException e) { System.out.println(e.getMessage()); }
        }
}
```

A shorter version of this program does not use the **myFile** object of class **File** , but instead uses the one-line expression   FileWriter fw = new FileWriter ("C:/JavaTextFiles/text_file_3.txt", true);

## 21.3. Reading from and writing into a text file in random order

We have seen how to read the content of a text file, from the beginning of the file all the way to the end, in a sequence. We have seen how to write into a text file, by appending information at the end of the file. Can we read from the text file, from any random position in the file? Can we write into the text file, at any random position in the file? The answer is yes, with the help of the **RandomAccessFile** class.

The **RandomAccessFile(File file, String mode)** constructor takes a **File** object, like before, together with a second parameter ( **"r"** for a read only text file, or **"rw"** when writing into the text file is allowed ) and instantiates a **RandomAccessFile** object. The methods of the **RandomAccessFile** class can read from or write into the random access text file at any place.

A random access file looks like a large 1D array of bytes. The same way we can access any byte in the array using an index, we can access any byte in the text file using a file pointer. We can find the value of the file pointer using the **long getFilePointer()** method, and we can change the value of the file pointer using the **seek(long fp)** method. The **long length()** method returns the length of the text file, which is the number of bytes stored in the file. The **setLength(long len)** method sets the length of the text file.

Reading from and writing into the random access file is done with a series of **read()** and **write()** method calls. After each **read()** or **write()** operation the file pointer is incremented, so we don't have to change the file pointer when we read or write in sequential order. When integer numbers that take two or more bytes are read or written, the high byte goes first.

The **int read()** method reads from the text file and returns an unsigned byte (a number in the 0 - 255 range), which is handled internally by Java as an **int** value, because Java does not have the unsigned byte among the primitive variable types. The method returns -1 when the end of the text file is reached.

The **boolean readBoolean()** method reads one byte from the text file , and then returns a **boolean** value. This return value is **false** when the byte is 0, and is **true** otherwise.

The **byte readByte()** method reads and returns a **byte** value.

The **char readChar()** method reads and returns a **char** value.

The **double readDouble()** method reads a **long** value from the text file, converts it to **double** , and then returns that **double** value.

The **float readFloat()** method reads an **int** value from the text file , converts it to **float** , and then returns that **float** value.

The **int readInt()** method reads and returns an **int** value.

The **long readLong()** method reads and returns a **long** value.

The **short readShort()** method reads and returns a **short** value.

The **String readLine()** method reads and returns a line of text (in ASCII format).

The **String readUTF()** method reads and returns a Unicode text string (in modified UTF-8 format).

The **write(int b)** method writes into the text file an unsigned byte (a number in the 0 - 255 range), which is handled internally by Java as an **int** value, because Java does not have the unsigned byte among the primitive variable types.

The **writeBoolean(boolean a)** method writes a byte (1 for **true** , 0 for **false**).

The **writeByte(int b)** method writes a **byte** value.

The **writeChar(int c)** method  writes a **char** value.

The **writeDouble(double d)** method converts the **double** input variable to **long** , and then writes into the text file that **long** value.

The **writeFloat(float f)** method converts the **float** input variable to **int** , and then writes into the text file that **int** value.

The **writeInt(int i)** method writes an **int** value.

The **writeLong(long j)** method writes a **long** value.

The **writeShort(int k)** method writes a **short** value.

The **writeLine(String s)** method writes a line of text (in ASCII format).

The **writeUTF(String s)** method writes a Unicode text string (in modified UTF-8 format).

When we are done with the random access file, we have to call the **close()** method, in order to save all the changes to the file, and free all the memory resources no longer needed.

The next program, Java Example 75, reads the **text_file_1.txt** file, which was created for the Java Example 72 program. Start NetBeans, as with the previous program, and in the **New Java Application** window type the **RandomFileRead** project name.

A shorter version of this program does not use the **myFile** object of class **File** , but instead uses the line RandomAccessFile raf = new RandomAccessFile ("C:/JavaTextFiles/text_file_1.txt", "rw");

Type the program, save the source file, and run the project.

```
// Java Example 75
package randomfileread;
import java.io.File;
import java.io.IOException;
import java.io.RandomAccessFile;

public class RandomFileRead
{

        public static void main(String[] args)
        {
                byte[] a = new byte[1000];

                try
                {
                        File myFile = new File("C:/JavaTextFiles/text_file_1.txt");
                        RandomAccessFile raf = new RandomAccessFile(myFile, "rw");
                        long len = raf.length();
                        System.out.println("The file length is : " + len);
                        raf.seek(0);
                        for (int i=0; i<=len; i=i+1) a[i] = (byte) raf.read();
                        raf.close();
                        for (int i=0; i<=len; i++) System.out.println(i + " " + a[i] + " " + (char) a[i]);
                        System.out.println("Text file read successfully.");
                } catch (IOException e) { System.out.println(e.getMessage()); }
        }
}
```

The text file is read one byte at a time, revealing the fact that the text was encoded using ASCII (American Standard Code for Information Interchange). The **text_file_1.txt** file was saved in this way in Notepad. For each byte in the text file, the program will print the file pointer (the index) of that byte, the numerical value of that byte (an ASCII code), and the ASCII alphanumeric character corresponding to that byte. The output from the program should look like this:

```
run:
The file length is : 99
0 102 f
1 105 i
2 114 r

97 120 x
98 116 t
99 -1 □
Text file read successfully.
BUILD SUCCESSFUL (total time: 0 seconds)
```

For a computer running the Windows operating system, the End Of Line (EOL) code consists of a pair of two characters : Carriage Return (CR , \r , ASCII code 13) and Line Feed (LF , \n , ASCII code 10). For a computer running UNIX the EOL code is just LF, while for a Macintosh computer the EOL code is just CR. The End Of File code (EOF, there is no ASCII code for it) is a negative number. The **read()** method returns -1 when it reads the EOF code, and this is the number printed out by the program. The length of the text file, as reported by the **length()** method, excludes the byte used by the EOF code.

Open the **text_file_1.txt** file in Notepad, and then save it ( File | Save As... ) using other available encodings : Unicode , Unicode big endian , UTF-8 . Run the Java Example 75 program again, to see the differences between the different encodings. A Unicode alphanumeric character takes two bytes. For the English alphabet one byte is the ASCII code and the other byte is 0 . For Unicode encoding the second byte is 0 , but for Unicode big endian encoding the first byte is 0 . For the English alphabet the UTF-8 encoding looks just like ASCII, it was designed like this in order to save space on the hard disk.

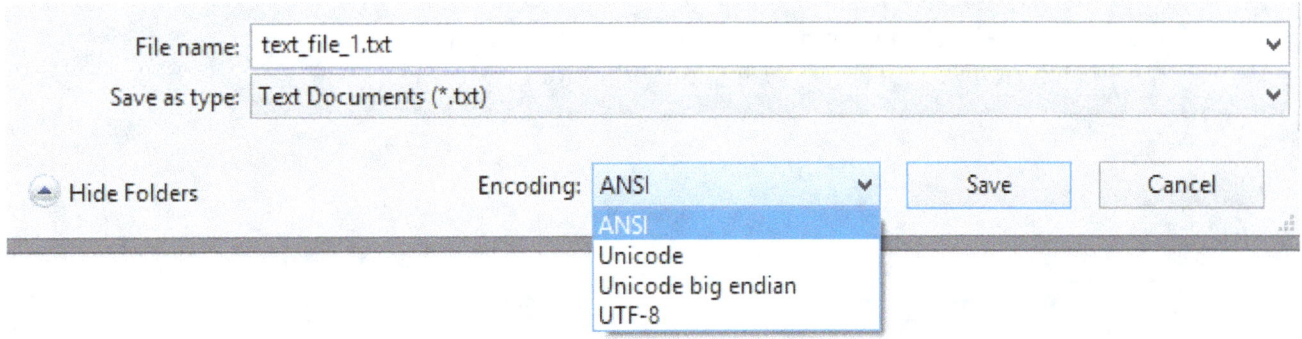

At the end of this activity, save the **text_file_1.txt** file using the ANSI encoding. We need the text file saved like this for the next exercise.

The next program, Java Example 76, will make some changes to the **text_file_1.txt** file.

Start NetBeans, as with the previous program, and in the **New Java Application** window type the **RandomFileWrite** project name. Type the program, save the source file, and run the project.

In the **text_file_1.txt** file the two words "first" (that started at a file pointer of 0) and "third" (that started at a file pointer of 41) should have swapped position. Open the **text_file_1.txt** file and check it. Close the text file. Run the program again. Open the **text_file_1.txt** file again and verify that the changes have been reversed.

```java
// Java Example 76
package randomfilewrite;
import java.io.File;
import java.io.IOException;
import java.io.RandomAccessFile;

public class RandomFileWrite
{

    public static void main(String[] args)
    {
        byte[] a = new byte[5];
        byte[] b = new byte[5];

        try
        {
            File myFile = new File("C:/JavaTextFiles/text_file_1.txt");
            RandomAccessFile raf = new RandomAccessFile(myFile, "rw");
            raf.seek(0);
            for (int i=0; i<5; i=i+1) a[i] = (byte) raf.read();
            raf.seek(41);
            for (int i=0; i<5; i=i+1) b[i] = (byte) raf.read();
            raf.seek(0);
            for (int i=0; i<5; i=i+1) raf.write(b[i]);
            raf.seek(41);
            for (int i=0; i<5; i=i+1) raf.write(a[i]);
            raf.close();
            System.out.println("Text file changed successfully.");
        } catch (IOException e) { System.out.println(e.getMessage()); }
    }

}
```

## 22. Quizmaker - an example of a useful Java application

We now look at a longer Java program, **Quizmaker** , an example of a Java program that has a useful purpose. Many of the Java programming concepts developed so far (with the help of short, simple Java Example programs) are now brought together, to make this useful Java application. This is how complexity increases in a system. In a similar way, with the help of many simple Lego bricks, you can build very complex structures. You may think of all the Java primitive variable types, classes, methods, and programming structures (that you have now mastered) as your Lego bricks. Build away - have fun programming!

The Java **Quizmaker** program will make a quiz with multiple choice (matching) questions. The program will also make the related answer key. The program starts by reading, from a text file, a list of questions and their answers. You can also have a list of keywords and their definitions, a vocabulary set in a foreign language, or any other kind of matching items.

Step 1. Go to the **C:\JavaTextFiles** folder.

Step 2. Inside the **JavaTextFiles** folder create a new text file. Right-click with the mouse, then select **New|Text Document**. Change the name of the file from **New Text Document.txt** to **Q_and_A.txt** .

Step 3. Using **Notepad**, open the **Q_and_A.txt** file, type the 24 lines of text shown on the next page, and then save the text file and close Notepad. Please notice that every question takes one line, every answer takes one line, and every answer follows its related question. The text file should look like this:

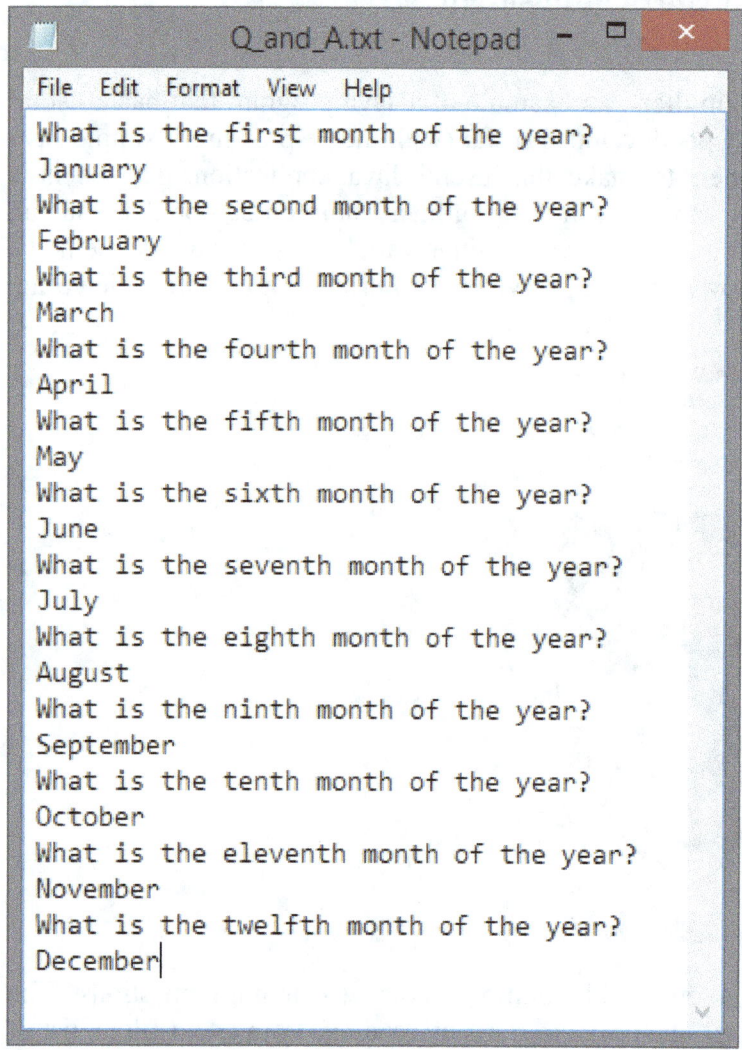

Step 4. Double click on the NetBeans shortcut link on the desktop.

Step 5. From the menu select **File|New Project...** or click on the **New Project** button.

Step 6. In the **New Project** window the **Java Application** option should be already selected. Click on the **Next** button.

Step 7. In the **New Java Application** window type the **Quizmaker** project name. The **Create Main Class** checkbox should be checked. Click on the **Finish** button.

Step 8. Delete all the comments that were automatically included in the Java program, and align the curly braces on the left side.

Step 9. Type the Quizmaker program listed on the next pages.

Step 10. Click on the Save All button.

Step 11. Click on the Run Project button.

// Quizmaker

```
package quizmaker;
import java.util.Scanner;
import java.io.File;
import java.io.IOException;
import java.io.FileReader;
import java.io.BufferedReader;
import java.io.FileWriter;
import java.io.BufferedWriter;
import java.util.ArrayList;
import java.util.Collections;

public class Quizmaker
{
    public static void main(String[] args)
    {
        String[] questions1 = new String[100];   // from the input text file
        String[] answers1 = new String[100];
        String[] questions2 = new String[100];   // after the first shuffle
        String[] answers2 = new String[100];
        String[] questions3 = new String[100];   // after the second shuffle
        String[] answers3 = new String[100];
        int nTotal = 0;   // the total number of questions in the input text file
        int nQuiz = 0;   // the number of questions in the quiz

        // READ THE QUESTIONS AND THE ANSWERS FROM A TEXT FILE
        Scanner kbdInput = new Scanner(System.in);
        System.out.println("What is the path name of the input text file?");
        String textfile1 = kbdInput.next();   // input : C:\JavaTextFiles\Q_and_A.txt

        try
        {
            File myFile1 = new File(textfile1);
            FileReader fr1 = new FileReader(myFile1);
            BufferedReader br1 = new BufferedReader(fr1);
            boolean Q = true;   // the first text line is always a question
            String textLine = br1.readLine();
            while (textLine != null)
            {
                if(Q)   // the text line is a question
                {
                    questions1[nTotal] = textLine;
                    Q = false;   // the next text line will be an answer
                }
                else   // the text line is an answer
                {
                    answers1[nTotal] = textLine;
                    Q = true;   // the next text line will be a question
                    nTotal = nTotal + 1;
```

```
      }
      textLine = br1.readLine();
   }
   br1.close();
   System.out.println("The text file has " + nTotal + " questions.");
} catch(IOException e) { System.out.println( e.getMessage() ); }

for(int i=0; i<nTotal; i=i+1)
{
   System.out.println(i + " " + questions1[i] + " " + answers1[i]);
}
System.out.println("How many questions are there in the quiz?");
nQuiz = kbdInput.nextInt();   // input : 7

// SCRAMBLE THE QUESTIONS AND THE ANSWERS
ArrayList<Integer> myList1 = new ArrayList<Integer>();
for(int i=0; i<nTotal; i=i+1) myList1.add(i);
Collections.shuffle(myList1);
System.out.println("myList1 after the shuffle : ");
for(int i=0; i<nTotal; i=i+1)
{
   int j = myList1.get(i);
   System.out.print(j + " ");
   questions2[i] = questions1[j];
   answers2[i] = answers1[j];
}
System.out.println();

ArrayList<Integer> myList2 = new ArrayList<Integer>();
for(int i=0; i<nQuiz; i=i+1) myList2.add(i);
Collections.shuffle(myList2);
System.out.println("myList2 after the shuffle : ");
for(int i=0; i<nQuiz; i=i+1)
{
   int j = myList2.get(i);
   System.out.print(j + " ");
   questions3[i]= questions2[i];
   answers3[i] = answers2[j];
}
System.out.println();

// WRITE THE QUIZ INTO A TEXT FILE
System.out.println("What is the path name of the text file with the quiz?");
String textfile2 = kbdInput.next();   // input : C:\JavaTextFiles\quiz.txt

try
{
   File myFile2 = new File(textfile2);
   FileWriter fw2 = new FileWriter(myFile2);
   BufferedWriter bw2 = new BufferedWriter(fw2);
```

```
         for(int i=0; i<nQuiz; i=i+1)
         {
            bw2.write(i+1 + ". ");
            bw2.write(questions3[i]);
            bw2.newLine();
         }
         bw2.newLine();
         for(int i=0; i<nQuiz; i=i+1)
         {
            bw2.write( (char)(65+i) + ". ");   // 65 is ASCII code for "A"
            bw2.write(answers3[i]);
            bw2.newLine();
         }
         bw2.close();
      } catch(IOException e) { System.out.println( e.getMessage() ); }

      // WRITE THE ANSWER KEY INTO A TEXT FILE
      System.out.println("What is the path name of the text file with the answer key?");
      String textfile3 = kbdInput.next();   // input : C:\JavaTextFiles\key.txt

      try
      {
         File myFile3 = new File(textfile3);
         FileWriter fw3 = new FileWriter(myFile3);
         BufferedWriter bw3 = new BufferedWriter(fw3);
         for(int i=0; i<nQuiz; i=i+1)
         {
            bw3.write(i+1 + " - ");
            for(int j=0; j<nQuiz; j=j+1)
            {
               if(i==myList2.get(j))
               {
                  bw3.write((char)(65+j));   // 65 is ASCII code for "A"
               }
            }
            bw3.newLine();
         }
         bw3.close();
      } catch(IOException e) { System.out.println( e.getMessage() ); }
   }
}
```

Step 11. Answer the questions asked by the running Quizmaker program.

Answer the first question with   **C:\JavaTextFiles\Q_and_A.txt**

Answer the second question with a number between 1 and 12. For my example, I used number 7.

Answer the third question with   **C:\JavaTextFiles\quiz.txt**

Answer the fourth question with   **C:\JavaTextFiles\key.txt**

A successful execution of the **Quizmaker** program will produce something like this:

```
run:
What is the path name of the input text file?
C:\JavaTextFiles\Q_and_A.txt
The text file has 12 questions.
0 What is the first month of the year? January
1 What is the second month of the year? February
2 What is the third month of the year? March
3 What is the fourth month of the year? April
4 What is the fifth month of the year? May
5 What is the sixth month of the year? June
6 What is the seventh month of the year? July
7 What is the eighth month of the year? August
8 What is the ninth month of the year? September
9 What is the tenth month of the year? October
10 What is the eleventh month of the year? November
11 What is the twelfth month of the year? December
How many questions are there in the quiz?
7
myList1 after the shuffle :
4 2 1 10 3 8 11 9 0 7 6 5
myList2 after the shuffle :
5 0 6 4 3 1 2
What is the path name of the text file with the quiz?
C:\JavaTextFiles\quiz.txt
What is the path name of the text file with the answer key?
C:\JavaTextFiles\key.txt
BUILD SUCCESSFUL (total time: 1 minute 56 seconds)
```

Step 12. Go to the **C:\JavaTextFiles** folder and make sure that two new text files, **quiz.txt** and **key.txt** , have been created. Open these two text files, using Notepad, and look at their content. You should see something like this:

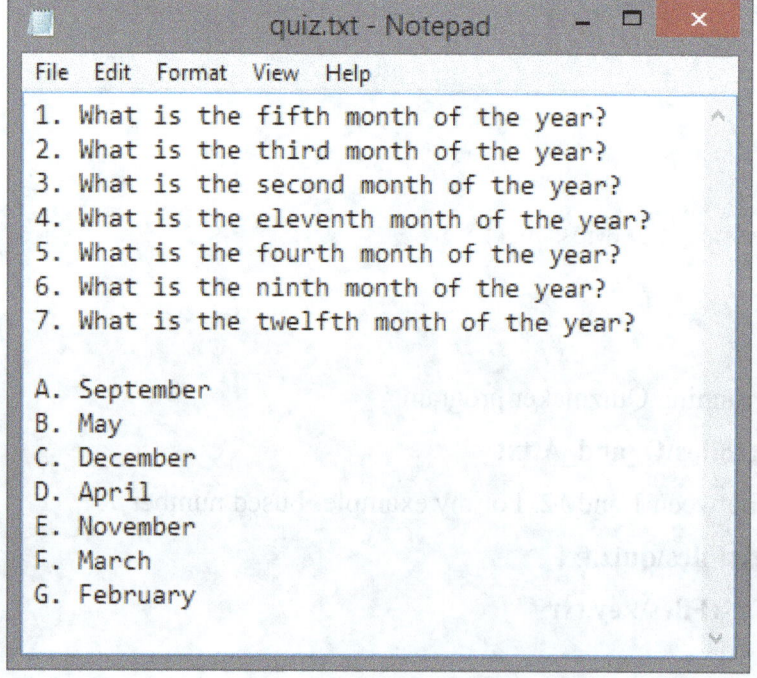

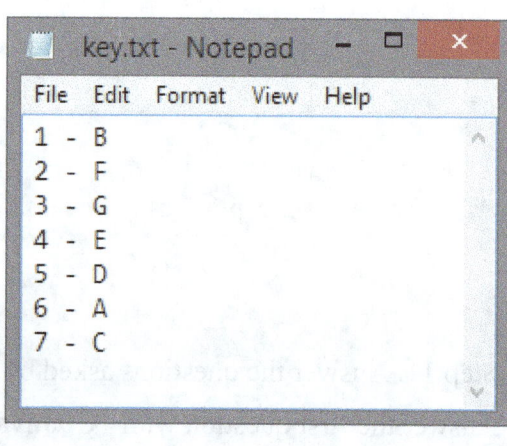

How does the **Quizmaker** program work? The **Quizmaker** program is modular, it has four main parts. These four parts, in the program listing, start at the comments in upper case letters.

In the first part, the program will read the questions and the answers from the input text file. The user has to give the path name (directory and file name) of the input text file. The text lines from this file are first read and then written into two **String** arrays, **questions1** for the questions and **answers1** for the answers. The program uses a **boolean** variable named **Q** in order to decide whether the most recently read text line is a question or an answer. While reading the questions and the answers, the program is also incrementing a counter, an **int** variable named **nTotal** , that starts equal to 0 and ends up equal to the total number of questions in the input text file. The program will also give some information to the user, printing the total number of questions, as well as all the questions and their answers. After this the user will give the number of questions in the quiz, information stored in an **int** variable named **nQuiz** .

In the second part, the program will randomly select **nQuiz** questions from the total of **nTotal** questions. This is done with the help of **myList1** , an **ArrayList** list of **Integer** objects. The **nTotal** integer numbers 0, 1, 2, ... , nTotal-1, corresponding to the different questions in the input text file, are scrambled using the **shuffle()** method. The scrambled questions are saved into the **questions2 String** array, and their answers are saved into the **answers2 String** array, in the same order. In other words, questions2[i] = questions1[j]; and answers2[i] = answers1[j]; , where j = myList1.get(i); .

Only the first **nQuiz** elements of the **questions2** and **answers2 String** arrays are then used to generate the quiz. After the random selection of the **nQuiz** questions, the program will scramble their answers. This is done with the help of a second **ArrayList** list of **Integer** objects named **myList2** . The **nQuiz** integer numbers 0, 1, 2, ... , nQuiz-1, corresponding to the different questions in the output text file, are scrambled using the **shuffle()** method once more. The unscrambled questions are saved into the **questions3 String** array, and their scrambled answers are saved into the **answers3 String** array. In other words, questions3[i] = questions2[i]; and answers3[i] = answers2[j]; , where j = myList2.get(i); .

To help you understand the process described above, we explicitly display the content of all these **String** arrays and **ArrayList** lists, as it happened during the trial run shown on the previous pages.

| i | questions1[i] | answers1[i] | j = myList1.get(i) |
|---|---|---|---|
| 0 | First month? | January | 4 |
| 1 | Second month? | February | 2 |
| 2 | Third month? | March | 1 |
| 3 | Fourth month? | April | 10 |
| 4 | Fifth month? | May | 3 |
| 5 | Sixth month? | June | 8 |
| 6 | Seventh month? | July | 11 |
| 7 | Eighth month? | August | 9 |
| 8 | Ninth month? | September | 0 |
| 9 | Tenth month? | October | 7 |
| 10 | Eleventh month? | November | 6 |
| 11 | Twelfth month? | December | 5 |

| i | questions2[i] | answers2[i] | j = myList2.get(i) |
|---|---------------|-------------|--------------------|
| 0 | Fifth month? | May | 5 |
| 1 | Third month? | March | 0 |
| 2 | Second month? | February | 6 |
| 3 | Eleventh month? | November | 4 |
| 4 | Fourth month? | April | 3 |
| 5 | Ninth month? | September | 1 |
| 6 | Twelfth month? | December | 2 |
| 7 | Tenth month? | October | |
| 8 | First month? | January | |
| 9 | Eighth month? | August | |
| 10 | Seventh month? | July | |
| 11 | Sixth month? | June | |

| i | questions3[i] | answers3[i] | i + 1 | (char) (65 + i) |
|---|---------------|-------------|-------|-----------------|
| 0 | Fifth month? | September | 1 | A |
| 1 | Third month? | May | 2 | B |
| 2 | Second month? | December | 3 | C |
| 3 | Eleventh month? | April | 4 | D |
| 4 | Fourth month? | November | 5 | E |
| 5 | Ninth month? | March | 6 | F |
| 6 | Twelfth month? | February | 7 | G |

In the third part, the program will write the quiz into the first output text file. The user has to give the path name (directory and file name) of the text file with the quiz. The program will just copy in order the questions from **questions3** and the answers from **answers3** . However, since we don't want the answers given to these matching questions to look like a spider web, it is recommended to label the questions with 1, 2, 3, 4, 5, 6, 7 and the answers with A, B, C, D, E, F, G. For this purpose the program uses the expression **i + 1** in front of the questions and the expression **(char) (65 + i)** in front of the answers. Here the **(char)** typecast operator turns an ASCII code into an upper case letter.

In the fourth part, the program will write the answer key into the second output text file. The user has to give the path name (directory and file name) of the text file with the answer key. The program will just copy in order the numbers **i + 1** representing the questions from **questions3** (same questions and in the same order as in **questions2** ), followed by the letter **(char) (65 + j)** representing the correct answer from **answers3** . The program has to unscramble the scrambled answers, this means it has to determine the value of **j** for each value of **i** .

The answer key to the quiz consists of all the questions from **questions2** (same questions and in the same order as in **questions3** ), followed by the correct answer found in **answers2** at the position with the same index **i** . However, the same correct answer must be found in **answers3** at the position with index **j** . In other words, for each **i** , **questions3[i] = questions2[i]** , and the correct answer is **answers2[i]** , which must be equal to **answers3[j]** , the correct answer listed in the answer key. We are therefore looking for the **j** value which solves the equation   **answers2[i] = answers3[j]**   .

When we have scrambled the answers, we have taken the answer from the position with index **j = myList2.get(i)**   in **answers2** and we have written it at the position with index **i** in **answers3** . In other words,   **answers3[i] = answers2[j]**   .

Let us now relabel the index variables. Instead of **i** we will write **j** , and instead of **j** we will write **i** . We can do that, **i** and **j** are dummy variables that take all the values from 0 to nQuiz-1 , and each **i** in this set is related to a **j** in the same set. The relations from the above paragraph become   **i = myList2.get(j)** and   **answers3[j] = answers2[i]**   . But this last equation is exactly the relation we were looking for! It happens when   **i = myList2.get(j)**   .

To summarize, for a question with position index **i** and number **i + 1** in the quiz, the answer is the letter **(char) (65 + j)** , where the value of **j** is the solution to the equation   **i = myList2.get(j)**   . The program solves this equation by guess and check, testing all the possible values of **j** until a match is found.

www.ingramcontent.com/pod-product-compliance
Lightning Source LLC
Chambersburg PA
CBHW081053170526
45165CB00006B/2262